FROM
THE METHODIST PULPIT
INTO
CHRISTIAN SCIENCE

AND

HOW I DEMONSTRATED THE ABUNDANCE OF SUBSTANCE AND SUPPLY

———

REVEREND SEVERIN E. SIMONSEN

NINTH EDITION

Robert H. Sommer
Publisher
Harrington Park, NJ 07640

ISBN 0-933062-29x
Printed in the United States of America

DEDICATED TO MY BELOVED WIFE

MARY ELIZABETH

WHO HAS BEEN ONE WITH ME IN MY
DEMONSTRATIONS

CONTENTS

FOREWORD

I F THE READER takes up this volume with the idea of finding in it the setting forth of an ism concerning Christian Science, he will be disappointed. Neither is its publication founded on any desire to add anything to Mrs. Eddy's published writings—that being impossible. It is published simply to make public and beneficial the experience of an earnest seeker of the Truth who applied the Principle discovered by Mrs. Eddy, and who had unfolded to him the solution of one of the most vital problems confronting mankind today, namely, that of demonstrating over lack and limitation into the glorious freedom of the abundance of substance and supply. For, in reality, the lack of a correct understanding of substance and supply is the food upon which sin and sickness thrive and is the foremost antagonist to the First and Great Commandment—*Thou shalt have no other gods before me.*

Furthermore, it is an humble and conscientious statement, not of a theory or an idea concerning what Christian Science can do, but it is the setting forth in a simple, concise, and loving manner, actual facts and experiences which have come into my life through faithful study, application, and practice of the Principle underlying the revelation granted to Mrs. Eddy, as set forth in her textbook, *Science and Health with Key to the Scriptures.* For it was from her writings that I gained a more comprehensive understanding of the true, spiritual import of the Bible, and how to interpret God's instructions to man. Thereafter the Bible became a never-failing source of enlightenment with signs following.

It is in the hope that my experience may become a real help to suffering humanity in solving their many life problems on a truly scientific basis; for I know from bitter personal experience what it means to try to work out one's life problems, and demonstrate substance and supply, without this clearer understanding of the Principle of all true being.

I have also experienced, and am experiencing the peace, joy, comfort, liberty, and happiness which forever flow from the realization this understanding affords in demonstrating over, not only the problems of sin and disease, but over lack, limitation, want and woe as well.

I trust that the volume may be received and accepted in the spirit animating its publication, permitting its contents to clearly elucidate the motive, namely, to lovingly point steadfastly to the door of opportunity all who are struggling to gain a clearer and more comprehensive understanding and realization of the power of Truth to destroy the illusion of lack and limitation, want and woe, and demonstrate, in their experience, the joy and peace made manifest in the abundance of substance and supply ever available.

SEVERIN E. SIMONSEN.

LOS ANGELES, CALIFORNIA
  NINETEEN TWENTY-SEVEN

CHAPTER I

MY HEALING IN CHRISTIAN SCIENCE

HE DAUNTLESS and heroic Vikings were my early ancestors. My father and mother were both Norsemen, descendants of the fearless Vikings who first discovered America in the year 1001 A.D. My parents set sail from Skein, Norway, in the Spring of 1843, and were among the first Viking descendants of that period to seek their homes in this new Land of Promise.

They took passage in a large government vessel known as a packet, which carried mail. Crossing the ocean in a palatial steamship was not in vogue at that time, although Samuel Cunard, the son of a Philadelphia merchant had begun to experiment along this line.

The voyage was an exceedingly long and tedious one. They were three weeks crossing the North Sea, and during this time encountered such stormy and tempestuous weather that the old packet sprung a leak, and they were forced to return to port twice in order to make repairs, that the vessel be made seaworthy.

They came by the way of Quebec, Canada, down the Great Lakes to Milwaukee, Wisconsin, which at that time was only a small town. It was on this lap of their journey by water that they suffered the greatest hardships. In Milwaukee, unable to decide which way to turn, they finally employed a drayman to haul their baggage into the wilderness of Wisconsin.

There were seven in the party, my mother, father, my eldest brother, mother's sister, her husband, their child, and a young man who was their traveling companion.

Going through the woods due west from Milwaukee for a distance of about twenty-seven miles, they came to a place since named Pine Lake, but now known as Nashotah Mission. Here the drayman unloaded their luggage and returned home, leaving the little band of pioneers alone in the wilderness. They were unable to speak a word of English, and their only possessions, after Father had paid the drayman, were the baggage they brought with them, and one dollar. For a few nights they were compelled to sleep in the open, with Indians all about them.

Among other things, my father was a carpenter, and having brought his tools with him, he soon built their first log-cabin. He was also a born mechanic, in reality a genius; for he could build a house, barn, or wagon; could make farm tools and machinery, as well as repair them; pour castings, even to the moulding of stoves, sleigh-bells, and many utensils; do all kinds of blacksmithing, and was an expert in making and repairing guns. He was also an excellent huntsman; so when they set out to go to this new and strange country, he brought with him his favorite gun and a fair supply of ammunition. This enabled him to quickly replenish their scant food supply by shooting wild game, which was plentiful in those days. The lakes, too, were teeming with fish eager to strike at almost any kind of bait.

No one knows the many hardships and deprivations the early settlers passed through. For some time Milwaukee, twenty-seven miles distant, was their nearest market. In order to reach there they had to go afoot and carry home all their groceries, dry goods, and needed necessities. But throughout it all they were happy and full of good cheer even when sickness overtook them.

When the men left the little cabin to go into the great forests to locate the most fertile and promising government land claims in that section, they found neither roads nor trails upon which to travel. They carried their axes with them, being forced to blaze a trail, which would enable them to return to their home and loved ones.

Gradually conditions became better, and Father found no difficulty in securing work as a mechanic—men of his ability being in great demand. This in turn enabled him to employ others to do most of the clearing and heavy farm work. He was frequently called to Milwaukee to work in the foundries and machine shops. During his absence Mother with her little family bravely met all the vicissitudes of their pioneer life.

There were a number of Indian tribes near, but my mother generously shared her scant supply of food with them, and they were very friendly. In fact there is no record of the redmen molesting the white settlers in Wisconsin.

Father frequently related in a most interesting manner, some of their many rich experiences during the early pioneer days. The manner in which he told them left one with the feeling that they had been happy days for him, and that he had enjoyed all of the struggles and hardships to which they had been subjected.

I was the youngest of eight children, all born and reared on our beautiful farm near Oconomowoc, Wisconsin, excepting my eldest brother, who was two years old when they came to America.

My parents were deeply religious, and both were faithful students of the Bible, which was the main textbook of our home. As children we were required to study the Bible, the Catechism, and Bible history. Each evening Mother read several chapters from the Bible, after which we had family prayer. Also in the morning, regardless of the pressing work of the day, the Bible was read and prayers offered before breakfast. In this way it was my good fortune to hear the Bible read through many times. Both my mother and father prayed at these family gatherings; and as the children became converted to God, they also joined in the prayers, so that it eventually took on the aspect of a small but thoroughly established prayer meeting. At each noon hour, and in the evening, Father read and studied a portion of the Bible aside from the reading in which the family took part.

Both of my parents were most conscientious in the spiritual development and religious training of their children, and as a result of this training and their godly example, they had the great joy of seeing every one of their children turn to God and faithfully serve Him.

Very often I would sit with Father and read aloud to him from the Bible and John Bunyan's "A Pilgrim's Progress." He made both most clear and interesting to me by explaining some of what I read, and answering the questions I asked him.

The thing of paramount importance to me was the healing of the sick by Jesus and his disciples. In my young mind I questioned why the sick were not healed now as they were then. When I asked Father concerning it, he explained to me that the Christian people generally hold the idea that the time for miracles has passed, but this did not seem right to him, for he could find nothing in the Bible to warrant such a conclusion. Consequently he always prayed for the sick as well as the sinful.

The hospitality of our home was always offered to the ministers of the Gospel who came to preach in our neighborhood. They were welcome to remain with us as long as their duties required them to stay. During these many visits, Father and the different clergymen would not only talk over the topics of the day, but they would discuss the teachings of Jesus Christ, and of the apostles, the various phases of the church and Biblical history, as well as the tenets of our own church, and those taught by the other denominations. This was most interesting and instructive to me. It was a liberal education in religious matters.

The first church in our section was a Lutheran Church which Father helped to organize. He also superintended the building of their first edifice to which he generously contributed. Later when the Methodists came, and he found their doctrine was more in accordance with his views, he withdrew from the Lutheran denomination and joined the Methodist Episcopal Church, becoming the largest contributor to the support of their ministers and to the building of their house of worship.

It was during the construction of this church that I received my first practical lesson on honesty. Father had allowed me to accompany him on his trip to procure lumber for use in the building of the new church. Often when he was required to go to the market, he would take me with him, and these drives were a source of great joy and inspiration to me, for he would talk to me of the Bible, of the way of salvation, and the importance of being honest and truthful. When we returned with the lumber, while it was being unloaded, Father carefully counted each board, and in doing so, found that he had been given two sidings more than he had paid for. He said nothing about it at the time, but on our next trip for lumber, immediately after he had exchanged greetings with the man from whom he had purchased it, he promptly told him he was indebted for the two sidings given by mistake. I was only a lad at the time, but the lesson was indelibly stamped upon my memory, as was the further fact that my father and mother were strictly truthful and upright in all their dealings. They were always patient, loving and self-sacrificing in dealing not only with their children, but with their neighbors as well. Their happy married life extended over fifty years. I never heard either one speak an unkind word to the other, and they lovingly confided in each other in everything. I never knew my father to use tobacco in any form or touch a drop of intoxicating liquor, and his language was always pure and free from guile. I feel most grateful to God for such devout, cheerful and consistent Christian parents, and for being reared and trained for my life work in such a clean and pure religious home.

One Easter season, when I was about nine years of age, stands out most clearly to me. Two ministers came to our house and spent several days with us. The younger of the two men took a deep interest in my brother and myself, and talked to us a great deal on the subject of religion, relating to us some of the interesting experiences of his life. He explained to us that he took everything to God in prayer, not only his sins and mistakes, but that if he was ill he would ask God to heal him; and that should he lose anything he would ask God to help him find it. This all made a deep impression on me, and that very day I had the opportunity to test it out myself. I was playing in my father's blacksmith shop, and in cutting off a piece of steel it flew over into another part of the shop, and I was unable to find it. I dropped on my knees, and in my childish way asked God to find it for me. When I had finished my prayer I found myself looking directly to where it lay. This pleased me greatly, and from that time on I took everything to God in prayer.

On my return from school one afternoon, I found my dear mother very ill, confined to her bed and suffeirng great pain. I immediately withdrew from her room, and going into the parlor I knelt down to ask God to heal her. I seemed ashamed to be found praying to God, so I knelt behind the door, prepared to rise quickly should any one enter the room, and be upon my feet before they could discover what I was doing. After I had prayed to God to heal Mother, I returned to her bedroom and found her up and dressing, as well and happy as usual. This and many other instances of God's answers to my prayers, greatly strengthened my faith in calling on Him for help in every hour of need.

One Sunday afternoon, when I was about thirteen years of age, I attended a prayer meeting at a neighbor's house with my father and mother and a brother about three years older than myself. Up to this time I had striven to lead a good, clean life. Nevertheless, that afternoon I was thoroughly awakened to three things: first,—the enormity of evil; second,—the dire consequences of evil; third,— the utter inability of evil to bring real peace, joy, pleasure or happiness to man. This in turn led me to truly repent of my sins and turn to my dear heavenly Father for my salvation from evil; consequently I was beautifully converted to God.

Although so young, my awakening, repentance, and conversion to God were deep and thorough— never to be repented of. I now became a devout and open professed follower of the Master, deeply interested in reading and studying the Bible.

It was not long, however, before the spirit of Truth and Love led me to see and realize and become thoroughly conscious of the fact that, in order to receive holiness, live it, and continue to walk therein, inasmuch as God was a holy God, and required His followers to be holy also, I must surrender my human will and all that pertained to me, as far as I understood it, to God unconditionally, as did Jesus our example, and to *fear God, and keep his commandments: for this is the whole duty of man.* (Eccles. 12:13.)

After much prayer and deep meditation, I came to the point where I not only clearly saw and realized that it was my duty as a Christian, but my privilege as a follower of Christ, to surrender and reconsecrate myself to God unconditionally.

I gladly took this forward step, and experienced what was known in the Methodist Church as "Sanctification." By sanctification I mean, as Webster defines it: "The act or process of God's grace by which the affections of man are purified or alienated from sin and the world and exalted to a supreme love of God."

The pure, sweet, and all-absorbing peace and joy of God that filled my whole being, as it were, is beyond human words. Living in this God-uplifted and supported state of mind, I came to see one day, as I was loading some hay on my father's farm, and thinking on the deeper things of God, that if I wished to continue to live in this glorious consciousness, and advance to still higher spiritual attainment I must watch my thoughts most carefully, and ever guard them, admitting only the good, the pure, and god-like. I therefore lovingly set myself to the task through prayer and God-inspired watchfulness.

Years later, when I discovered that this was one of the cardinal points in Christian Science, I was deeply grateful to my dear heavenly Father that He had graciously revealed this to me, and lovingly enabled me to put it into practice. This blessed experience occurred less than three years after I was converted to God.

It was not long after this when I first heard the "still small voice" of God calling to me to bring His message of love and salvation to mankind. I was deeply conscientious, however, in every important move I made, and I hesitated to even dare to think I was called to be a messenger of the Most High. I therefore said nothing about it to anyone except my heavenly Father. I did venture though, to hold services, and preach the Gospel of Christ to the best of my ability.

The first service I conducted was a prayer meeting six miles from my home, and I was compelled to walk there and back. The following Sunday, I spoke in the Methodist Church my father had helped to establish.

Our pastor had suddenly passed on, and I was sent to Milwaukee to secure a minister to conduct the funeral services. The Presiding Elder sent a man back with me, who before returning to Milwaukee, sought me out and asked me to take the pulpit, and preach until we were supplied with a minister.

It was with fear and trembling that I undertook this work. In the congregation were many boys with whom I attended school. It occurred in the early summer when we were repairing the public highways in our district, and I knew the following day would find me working on the roadway, and I would, in all probability, be subjected to their taunts. Each farmer in those days was taxed a certain sum for the building of the highways. He could pay his tax in money, or was privileged to have his men work it out, receiving so much allowance for the daily service of each man, span of horses, and the wagon. Father had chosen to contribute his share by our services. Sure enough, what I feared came upon me; but nothing daunted me, for God was with me, and He supported me beautifully.

I continued to preach until my elder brother and a young man friend with whom he was attending college, returned home for their summer vacation; and inasmuch as they were preparing to enter the active ministry, I thought perhaps I had better step aside, which I did, and they conducted the meetings throughout the summer.

When they returned to school in the fall, I again took over the work; but there were circumstances which indicated that it would have been better had I carried on the work intrusted to me by my dear heavenly Father. It taught me a useful lesson, however, which was that one should never turn over to another the work which God has intrusted to him; for whenever one attempts anything like that, he will find that he is apt to miss the blessing and reward for good and faithful work and unquestioning obedience to God.

When Moses hesitated and began to make excuses to God, when He called him to go and deliver the Children of Israel from the hands of Pharaoh, God sent Moses' brother, Aaron, with him to share in the work and the honor of the deliverance of God's chosen people.

It is imperative that we know just what God wants us to do, and then do it to the best of our ability and understanding, leaving the responsibility with God where it belongs.

Shortly after this incident, while working with my father in his carpenter shop, turning the grindstone, he suddenly asked me if I did not feel called to preach. His question startled me, as he seemed to sense the mental battle going on in my mind at the time, as to whether God was calling me to preach His word, or not. In my seeming confusion of thought, I quickly replied that I did not think this could be possible, inasmuch as my brother was preparing himself to enter the ministry. Father answered and told me he saw no reason why I should not also enter this sacred work, adding that he thought I was both qualified for and adapted to the work.

Sometime later I attended the Quarterly Conference, which was in session about ten miles from our home. There, without my knowledge, the Conference voted to grant me a license to preach.

Driving home alone that evening, along the country road in the quiet of the moonlight night, I knelt on the floor of the buggy, and asked God to show me what He wanted me to do. The next day while plowing, the same as Elisha, the son of Shaphat, did when he decided to heed God's call to become one of His prophets (I Kings 19:19), I stopped my work and going to a corner of the fence I again beseeched Him to make clear to me if He had really called me. It was that morning that I became thoroughly convinced I was called by God to preach and teach the Gospel of Christ; and in the evening while searching the Bible for added proofs, I came to two passages, which at this moment I do not recall, but which absolutely confirmed my decision.

However, another problem confronted me. I was the youngest of the children. Both my parents were along in years, and I was the only child at home, and apparently their mainstay. It appeared to me that it was my work to help them by looking after the farm, and I did not see how they could get along without me.

It was some time before I could bring myself to ⁺ell either of them; but one day, while driving home from town with Mother, I confided in her. To my surprise she told me she was very glad and proud to have three sons chosen for the ministry (the third son was my eldest brother. While in college preparing for the ministry, his health gave way, and he was obliged to give up this sacred calling. Later when he regained his health he became a successful business man.) She said she had been praying to God that if it were His will, I would be led to make such a choice. I asked her how they would get along without my help, and she answered me, just as she had often replied when other problems confronted her, "God will care for us."

But to tell Father was, it seemed, a different matter. He was getting old, and was, I felt, not able to take over the cares of the farm. It seemed cruel to leave them, and although I felt distinctly that it was my life-work to preach, I was reluctant to take up the subject with him.

Late in the fall of that year, Father and I were busy working in a gravel-pit, loading gravel to be used in the construction of a private road down through the meadows. The gravel-pit and road were quite symbolical of the problem before me, for surely deep down in the pit signified the depth of the mental state I seemed to be in. Yet I was sure of the road I wished to aid in building—God's highway, and lovingly help my fellow man to discern and walk thereon; the road Isaiah pictured and wrote of thus: *And an highway shall be there, and a way, and it shall be called The way of holiness; the unclean shall not pass over it; but it shall be for those: the wayfaring men, though fools, shall not err therein. No lion shall be there, nor any ravenous beast shall go up thereon, it shall not be found there; but the redeemed shall walk there:* (Isaiah 35: 8, 9). But my seeming mental agitation was over as to how my good father would view the situation.

I should have realized, however, how utterly groundless my fears were, because my dear father had lovingly inquired many months before if I did not feel that I was called to preach God's word, and frankly explained to me that he thought I was well adapted for this work. As I look back upon the fear and agitation of that day, what a clear illustration it brings forth; for when we allow error to talk to us it will invariably try to mislead us.

Finally, after much hesitation, I explained to him how God had called me to be one of His messengers, and then waited expectantly for what he might have to say. Very quickly he answered me. "I have long expected this," he said; and then he enquired if I wished to go at once to Evanston, where my brother was attending college, and take up the studies preparatory to entering the active ministry. I informed him that I thought it would be a better plan to do what studying I could at home until the next fall, as it seemed too late in the school year to enter at that time. He agreed with me, and generously offered the necessary funds whenever I saw fit to go. I was greatly relieved in mind, and happy in an added proof of God's goodness to me.

I now took up the study of the Scriptures with renewed energy, and the one burden of my heart was that I might know God better, serve Him more acceptably each day, be better qualified to be a servant of His, and to be of the greatest possible service to my fellow man. I therefore earnestly and prayerfully endeavored to place myself, and all that pertained to me, on God's altar unreservedly.

It was not long, however, before I was put to a test, in this way: in my early years, Father never allowed us to have a dog; but when I was about fifteen years old, I was permitted to secure a fine foxhound, which was one of the things I had longed to possess. After I had decided to preach I realized the possibility of my dog carrying me off on hunting trips, and I would be using the time hunting the fox which should be devoted to the study of the Scriptures in preparation for the services I was to conduct. I thought it over very seriously, and prayed earnestly to God that I might know what I should do in the matter, whether to keep the dog or dispose of him. I did so want to keep the dog, and yet if it were not right and best for me to do so, I had come to the place where I was willing to give him up. I called to my father, and asked him if he would not take the dog and dispose of him. Then I went on with my work rejoicing over the sacrifice, as it appeared to me, I, a young boy, had made.

Later I found Father had done nothing about the dog, neither was anything said. Mentally I had made the sacrifice, the same as Abraham had done when he was offering up Isaac. *And the angel of the Lord called unto him out of heaven, and said, Abraham, . . . Lay not thine hand upon the lad, neither do thou anything unto him: for now I know that thou fearest God, seeing thou hast not withheld thy son, thine only son from me* (Gen. 22: 11, 12). I was allowed to keep my pet, and my spare time was spent, instead of on hunting expeditions, in the study of the Scriptures, and the preparation for a higher service to mankind.

From the time I began to preach at the age of sixteen, I searched and studied the Scriptures faithfully, and I became more and more convinced that we were not carrying out the Master's command to heal the sick, as well as to save the sinner from his sins.

I frequently asked the ministers and my theological professors why we did not heal the sick in Jesus' way; but they replied, "Mr. Simonsen, the time for miracles has passed. The Christian religion is so well established now that we do not need these proofs any longer." Yet throughout it all this answer did not satisfy me, and I continued to earnestly search the Scriptures for an answer to this great question.

After I graduated from the Garrett Biblical Institute, in 1881, I spent more than a year abroad studying and preparing myself more fully for the ministry. While in Europe, I searched for someone who healed the sick according to Christ's command, but I could find no one. I did, however, learn of a man who had a sort of "Faith Cure" establishment, but after looking into the basis of it, I found that it was simply an effort to heal the sick through blind faith, and this did not seem in accord with my understanding of the Christ healing.

On my return to America, in 1882, I entered the active ministry of the Methodist Episcopal Church, and my first charge was in Stoughton, Wisconsin.

During my vacations, while preparing for the ministry, I traveled for a portrait company located in Chicago, Illinois, taking orders for the enlarging of photographs in india ink, water colors, and oil in order to pay my own way through school at Evanston. Although my good father stood ready to finance me, I deemed it wise to work during my vacations and pay my own way, for I was planning to go abroad to study after I had graduated, and to use Father's proffered money for this purpose, which I did.

In the summer of 1878, I canvassed the well-to-do farmers in Waukesha County, Wisconsin; and early one afternoon in June. I called at the beautiful home of ex-State Senator Parker Sawyer in Summit. I rang the front door bell, and as I stood there waiting to be admitted, I looked through the glass door and saw their youngest daughter, Mary Elizabeth, sitting at her grand piano, so deeply engrossed in the music she was playing that she did not notice the doorbell at all. A wave of disappointment swept over my mind as I stood there waiting and wondering if I, an agent, might ring her bell the second time. I concluded not to disturb her so I crossed over their broad veranda, and stepped down on the lawn toward my carriage to proceed on my journey, when Mr. Sawyer, who was busy at the pump a short distance away, noticed me and came to my rescue. He greeted me very cordially, and when he learned who I was, and of my errand, he at once expressed kindly interest; for he too, in early life had canvassed, and knew from personal experience something of the vicissitudes of an agent's life. But aside from this, he was greatly interested in encouraging and aiding young men who were preparing to preach the Gospel of Christ. He was himself a deep theological student and an elder in the Christian Church. He thereupon invited me into his home, remarking as we entered, that he personally knew little concerning art, but his daughter did, and was much interested in the subject.

On entering their front parlor, he called to his beautiful daughter who was still busy playing, and stated that he wished to introduce to her a young theological student from Evanston, who was canvassing for an art company in Chicago. While my call did not result in an order for an enlargement of their photographs, I accomplished something far greater than that: I succeeded in winning the love, heart, and hand of the best and dearest girl I have ever met. It was a case of love at first sight.

Mr. Sawyer knew so well what it meant to canvass in the country, and the difficulty of securing a midday meal, that after we had talked about works

of art for a time, he inquired if I had had any dinner that day; and when he learned that I had not,
he at once found his good wife, and after he introduced me to her, he asked her if she would not
kindly prepare a little lunch for me, which she did
very lovingly while father Sawyer put up my horse
and fed it. When he learned more of my mission in
life, and we found that we had mutual friends in
the neighborhood, he insisted that I spend some
time with them. They all made me feel so at home,
and made everything so interesting and inviting,
that I spent the entire afternoon with them.

After lunch, Miss Sawyer and I enjoyed several
games of croquet on their spacious lawn, but I
must confess that I was no match for her in playing
them. She won every game. My happiness, however, was unaffected, and I enjoyed it hugely. After
we had played for some time, we took a stroll down
to a beautiful little lake that skirted their farm, to
enjoy a boat ride; but on reaching the boat landing,
we found that the boat which was only partly on
the water had sprung a leak in one or two places.
At once I busied myself in caulking up the cracks
the best I could, submerging it in the water to soak
for a bit,—for an opportunity of a boat-ride on this
little gem of a lake with such a lovely young lady
was not to be missed. Just how long it took for the

bottom of the boat to swell enough to stop the leak-
ages so we could enjoy a ride in comfort, I do not
recall; but I know it seemed awfully short. I found
that Miss Sawyer had been a member of her college boat team, and was quite an expert rower. We
had a delightful time, and a very interesting boat-
ride.

When I drove away late in the afternoon, I did
not make any more calls for orders in oil that day;
my thoughts were too much accupied with my new-
found "pearl of great price." After this and for a
number of years afterwards I was a frequent caller.
We always had a most delightful visit together, and
after I had graduated and had finished my studying
abroad, and we were perfectly satisfied with our
undying love for each other, we became engaged.

Mrs. Simonsens' parents were also among the
early settlers of Wisconsin, having migrated from
Vermont. They were devout Christians. Father
Sawyer was an unusually well-read man, and one
of his several activities was the representation of
his district in the State Legislature for a number of
years. Her mother was a granddaughter of Ebe-
nezer Andrews of Fort Ticonderoga fame. She
came into Christian Science through my healing.
They had four children—two daughters and two
sons. One son was a Congregational minister, and

the other was a successful physician. The entire family was musical, but especially was this true of the daughters.

Mrs. Simonsen's sister was an unusually talented singer, pianist, and painter. She studied music in Leipsig Conservatory, Germany, and in Florence, Italy, after having graduated in this country. Mrs. Simonsen was the youngest of the family. She received her early education in a private school in Oconomowoc, and later attended colleges situated in Milwaukee, Wisconsin; Indianapolis, Indiana, and Lexington, Kentucky; completing her studies at the Howland School for Girls in Union Springs, New York.

After Mrs. Simonsen finished her work at the Howland School, she returned to her home and devoted her time to the teaching of music in Oconomowoc until we were happily married in the early spring of 1883, in her lovely home and on the very spot where we first met. After a brief but happy honeymoon we settled in my new parish in Stoughton, Wisconsin.

While in Stoughton I was requested to write a paper for our District Conference on the subject, "Is the Time for Miracles Past?" This gave me a splendid opportunity to study this interesting topic anew, and to go into it more thoroughly than I had been able to do until this time. The more deeply I studied the Scriptures on the subject, the more convinced I became that Christ's command was perpetual,—for all time, and for all people. Although I consulted all the best available authors, I cannot recall a single writer who could get away from the old threadbare conclusion that the time for miracles had passed. Furthermore, they could only advance two major reasons, namely, "The Christian religion was now so well established throughout the world that we did not need this line of proof to demonstrate the power of God"; and in the second place, "We have hospitals well equipped with doctors, surgeons, nurses, and medicines to care for the sick and suffering." As I was at this time fast losing my own health, in spite of all the good doctor could do, these theories were of poor comfort to me. I finally concluded that according to the Bible, the time for miracles had not passed, although according to our best theologians, it had. So I left it there.

My next pastorate was in La Crosse, Wisconsin. Here my health, which had been poor for more than a year, caused me to have a complete breakdown, and although I sought the help of many of the leading physicians in that section of the country, I continued to grow steadily worse, until they frankly told me there was no hope for me, and that

I could live only two or three months longer. One said I might perhaps linger on for a year if I could live out of doors in the northern part of Wisconsin— in the West Superior region. I explained to him I was not in a position financially to do so, and also that I had a wife and two children to care for; but all they seemed able to do, was to shake their heads sagely, and tell me they had done for me all they could do. One dear old doctor continued to come in to see me several times each day. He was an engaging old gentleman, and at times related to us many of his interesting experiences with the sick. One related was how he had his own sister sick abed by only looking at her tongue, feeling her pulse, and telling her how ill she looked; and then how he cured her by giving her pellets made of bread that did not contain any medicine. But he was unable to do anything for me even with real medicine.

A sense of despair settled down on me more and more each day. I did so want to live for my family, and carry on my work for the Master, but I saw no way to recover my health and strength, and I felt that I would have to be reconciled to passing on.

While I was in this desperate condition Christian Science was first brought to my attention. Strange to relate, the messenger was a Methodist Minister and theological professor--my elder brother. The professor had a good friend who had been marvelously healed through Christian Science, and suggested I try it. Before doing so, I talked with my brother-in-law, who was a practicing physician, and asked him about Christian Science, for I had no knowledge of it whatsoever. The doctor assured me, although he knew nothing about it, that it was nothing but hypnotism; so I dismissed the subject from my mind for the time being. This was forty-one years ago—when Christian Science was in its infancy in the Middle West—and I had never seen the textbook or read a word on the subject.

Early in the year 1886, the Official Board of the church I was serving kindly granted me an extended leave of absence, in the hope that it might help me in my effort to regain my health. The church members were very kind to me, and did all they could to make it as pleasant as possible under the circumstances.

One evening a member called on me, and asked me to try Christian Science. I told her I would have nothing to do with it, and that I had no money to throw away on such experiments. She then wanted to know if I did not recall visiting Mrs. R—, about a year before, when she sat in a morris chair, a helpless invalid, paralyzed in her right side; I said,

"Yes, I remember the lady well." Then my friend went on and said, "Mrs. R— has been beautifully healed through Christian Science, has been in Boston studying, and is home now, a well woman, and is healing people through Christian Science. I have told her about you, and that the doctors have all given you up; and she said she saw no reason why you, too, could not be healed." I told her again, I would have nothing to do with it; and added, "If God did not answer the prayers of my good family and my church members, nor my own constant pleadings for help, I cannot see why He would intervene and help me just because a Christian Scientist asked Him to do so."

The good lady said nothing further on the subject that night; but when she called again in less than two weeks and found me fast slipping away, she made brave to bring up the subject again. By now, I was so far gone that I was willing to try anything that I thought might help me; and when she once more asked me to try Christian Science, I grasped at it as a drowning man grasps at a straw.

The next day I managed to get out in my carriage and drive over to the practitioner. She lived on the same street, and only a few doors from where my friend, the doctor lived. Somehow I did not wish to have him know I had decided to try

Christian Science. Therefore I deliberately hitched my horse a few doors from where she lived, and before I walked up to her door I took a careful survey of the people on the street to make sure that no one was in sight who personally knew me. I was relieved when her door opened and I found myself safely inside.

This occurred at eleven o'clock Saturday morning. I shall never forget it. It was the beginning of better things for me. The practitioner was very cautious, and told me only a few plain facts about Christian Science, and that a patient must abstain from using any and all material means while under treatment. She sat comfortably in a large easy chair, with her eyes closed as she treated me for about twelve minutes.

I am free to confess I was very much disappointed in this quiet way of doing things. I had expected her to drop on her knees and "wrestle mightily with God," as we Methodists used to say, when something so unusual was going to take place as the healing of a Methodist minister who had besought the good Lord day and night for several years to heal him.

But I had many important lessons to learn; and one was that *the Lord was not in the wind; . . . not in the earthquake: . . . not in the fire:* but in the *still small voice* (I Kings 19:11, 12). I said nothing to her of my thought and feelings at that time, but after I was healed I told her about the amusing incident. I felt no perceptible change or effect from the treatment at the time; in fact I thought to myself that after all, there was nothing to Christian Science or its treatments, and that the effort was simply another failure in my endeavor to regain my health.

When the practitioner said good-bye to me, she told me I could eat anything I cared for; and if I wished to go into my pulpit and preach the next morning, I could do so. God would care for me. I said nothing, but only looked pityingly at her, and in my heart I thought, "You poor deluded soul; how little you comprehend my condition."

As I stepped out upon her porch, I suddenly glanced up and down the street to see if my good doctor should be outside his home, or any of my church members, by chance, be passing by; but the road was clear, and I managed to reach my carriage and home without being discovered so far as I knew.

As I was taking another mental inventory, my good, faithful, and ever-inspiring wife came to me, and assured me that I looked better. When I told her the healer had said I could eat anything I wished—for a long time past I could scarcely eat anything—she at once betook herself to the market, and it was not long before I was invited to partake of one of the most savory meals I have ever had placed before me. She had prepared a thick, juicy porterhouse steak—cooked just right, potatoes, stewed corn, bread, butter, coffee and dessert. What more could a man wish for? I ate a generous portion of everything, . . . *asking no questions for conscience sake:* and I never felt better after any meal in my life.

The following day was a glorious one for me. I felt like a new man; and I realized that a better understanding of God and man, of God's relationship to man, and man's relationship to God was dawning upon me. When I turned to my Bible and read it, the book opened up to me with a clearer illumination than ever before. I went into my pulpit that morning, much to the amazement of my good people, and I preached with greater liberty, and with the glorious consciousness of the presence of God. The deep and absorbing interest with which my congregation drank in this new, yet old message of Truth and Love that was unfolding to me, is still very vivid in my memory.

I was passing through an experience and unfoldment never to be forgotten. Everything—God, man, and all nature,—took on a more glorious appearance. My work at once became a greater joy to me than it had ever been, and I found as my day was, so was my strength; for Christian Science was enlightening me from whence came my strength, wisdom, and love.

But who was Mrs. Eddy? What was the Truth she had given to the world, and which had wrought such a marvelous change in me, not only physically, but mentally as well; also this broader, better, and clearer view of God, man, and the universe which was now being unfolded to me? I must know.

CHAPTER II

N CARRYING OUT His plan of salvation, God
has always selected the individual and
the people who were best fitted for His
chosen messengers to the rest of mankind. For instance, He selected Abraham and his
seed to be His chosen people to receive His revelation, which in turn would reach all mankind.

When the children of Israel needed a deliverer
from their bondage in Egypt, God sent His servant
Moses, whom He had long been preparing for the
great task that lay before him. Is it not fair then,
to assume that Moses was by all means the best and
in every way the most suitable man in all the world
for this important mission? If there had been a
better man anywhere, would not God have chosen
him for this work? Is not this true also of all great
leaders and prophets of both the Old and New
Testament times? It seems so to me.

If there had been, using another illustration, a

man better equipped, better trained, more spiritually minded, and more devoted to God and His people than Daniel, would he not have been found by the all-seeing and all-knowing God of Israel; and would he not have been called to be the messenger of the Most High, and to receive the revelation that God revealed to His servant Daniel?

Again, in the fulness of time, when God sent His only-begotten Son into the world, He selected one of the seed of Abraham to be the mother of Jesus, and why? Because, in His infinite wisdom, He saw in this seed the best element among all mankind; for in Mary He found the most spiritually minded, gentle, and best equipped of all women. If this had not been true, the All-knowing would not have selected Mary.

The appearance of the Messiah was, of course, at the most opportune time; for when the angel appeared unto Mary, it is an historical fact that the world was ready for the appearance of the Messiah. The Roman Empire had extended over the then civilized world, unifying the nations of all mankind, thus facilitating the spread of the Gospel. The mass of the common people, Jew and Gentile alike oppressed by the harsh rule, were unconsciously yearning for a new revelation of God which would bring them deliverance and peace.

Later, when the children of God's chosen race, in their wilful ignorance of the Messiah, refused to receive him, and the Gentiles were ready to listen to and receive the glad Gospel of Jesus Christ, God selected Saul of Tarsus to be His standard bearer among the Gentiles. Of His selection we read in Romans this statement: *Paul, a servant of Jesus Christ, called to be an apostle, separated unto the gospel of God . . . by whom we have received grace and apostleship, for obedience to the faith among all nations, for his name.* Today we know from his record and copious writings that he was the best man among all men for this important mission.

The Christ-healing of the sick and the suffering as inaugurated by Jesus, and carried on by his disciples, was early lost sight of. When the Christian Church and its ministry ceased to carry out the whole of Christ's command to preach the Gospel and heal the sick, the church soon lapsed into formalism and worldliness. Then it was not long before the Dark Ages settled over the Christian World, which continued for centuries until such messengers of God as Martin Luther, Melancthon, John Huss, John Knox, John Wesley and others proclaimed the Gospel of healing from sin: and while the Christian Church took a fresh start, and did much to release mankind from the thraldom of sin, it did little or nothing in the line of healing the sick and suffering in Christ's way.

When the time came for the reappearing of the Gospel of Christ in its fulness, and the world was ready for the revelation of Christian Science, God in His infinite wisdom, selected as His messenger and standard bearer of the divine Science, one from the American people, one from a nation which today stands for the highest ideals known to mankind, and from a people to whom the suffering and sin-sick world is looking for succor from its miseries. This God-chosen American is known to all the world today as Mary Baker Eddy.

In the year 1866, Mary Baker Eddy appeared upon the religious horizon as the Discoverer and Founder of Christian Science, and in 1875, as the Author of its textbook, *Science and Health with Key to the Scriptures.* This American woman with her training, ability, mental and spiritual unfoldment, as well as her purity, unselfishness, and consecration to God and the good of all mankind, must necessarily have been the most suitable in all the world to be God's messenger to this age, or He would never have chosen her. God never makes a mistake.

In the study of God's messengers, we find that they were required to give ample proof of their high calling. Moses, for instance, had to prove to the children of Israel that the great I AM had sent him to deliver them from the Egyptians and their bondage.

In the fourth chapter of Exodus we read: *And Moses answered* [God] *and said, But, behold, they will not believe me, nor hearken unto my voice: for they will say, The Lord hath not appeared unto thee. And the Lord said unto him, What is that in thine hand? And he said, A rod. And he said, Cast it on the ground. And he cast it on the ground, and it became a serpent; and Moses fled from before it. And the Lord said unto Moses, Put forth thine hand, and take it by the tail. And he put forth his hand, and caught it, and it became a rod in his hand: That they may believe that the Lord God of their fathers, the God of Abraham, the God of Isaac, and the God of Jacob, hath appeared unto thee. And the Lord said furthermore unto him, Put now thine hand into thy bosom. And he put his hand into his bosom: and when he took it out, behold, his hand was leprous as snow. And he said, Put thine hand into thy bosom again. And he put his hand into his bosom again; and plucked it out of his bosom, and, behold, it was turned again as his other flesh. . . . And the Lord said unto Moses, When thou goest to return into Egypt, see that thou do all those wonders before Pharaoh, which I have put in thine hand. . . . And the Lord said to Aaron, Go into the wilderness to meet Moses. . . . And Moses told Aaron all the words of the Lord who had sent him, and all the signs which he had commanded him. And Moses and Aaron went and gathered together all the elders of the children of Israel: . . . and did the signs in the sight of the people. And the people believed: and when they heard that the Lord had visited the children of Israel, and that he had looked upon their afflictions, then they bowed their heads, and worshipped.*

After Moses had thus established in the minds of the people that he was sent of God to deliver them, he went in unto Pharaoh and demanded that he let the children of Israel go; and when Pharaoh demurred and wanted to know who he (Moses) was, he gave unto Pharaoh the proofs necessary to establish the fact that he was God's chosen messenger; and he succeeded and delivered God's chosen people from their bondage in Egypt.

Even Jesus the Christ had to give ample proof that he was the promised Messiah. In fact it was prophesied centuries before his appearing on the plains of Judea just what proofs he would give of his claim to his Messiahship.

The prophet Isaiah wrote: *Strengthen ye the weak hands, and confirm the feeble knees. Say to*

*them that are of a fearful heart, Be strong, fear not.
. . . He will come and save you. Then the eyes of
the blind shall be opened, and the ears of the deaf
shall be unstopped. Then shall the lame man leap
as an hart, and the tongue of the dumb sing.* And
when the Christ appeared centuries afterwards
these were the very signs whereby he established
that he was the Son of God; and they were the only
proofs, he explained to the people, whereby they
might know if a messenger were sent of God or not.

When John the Baptist sat in prison because he
had rebuked the sensuous Herod, he had time for
reflection on some of his work in the past, and on
the different men he had baptized. There was one
man whom he had baptized in Jordan, who loomed
up before him as an unusual character; for he had
seen the dove descending upon him, and heard the
voice of God saying, *This is my beloved Son, in
whom I am well pleased.* Yet he was not quite sure
that this man was the promised Messiah.

John therefore sent two of his disciples to Jesus
with this question: *Art thou he that should come,
or do we look for another? Jesus answered and said
unto them, Go and show John again those things
which ye do hear and see: The blind receive their
sight, and the lame walk, the lepers are cleansed,
and the deaf hear, the dead are raised up, and*

the poor have the gospel preached to them. And blessed is he, whosoever shall not be offended in me.

Jesus did not refer John to any particular doctrine or set of theological beliefs in establishing his Messiahship, not one. He rested his claim on the unfailing signs of a true messenger of God, which he had already specified in his Sermon on the Mount, when he warned all men of all ages to *Beware of false prophets, which come to you in sheep's clothing, but inwardly they are ravening wolves.* He said: *Ye shall know them by their fruits. Do men gather grapes of thorns, or figs of thistles? Even so every good tree bringeth forth good fruit; but a corrupt tree bringeth forth evil fruit. A good tree cannot bring forth evil fruit, neither can a corrupt tree bring forth good fruit. . . . Wherefore by their fruits ye shall know them.*

These sure and unfailing signs of one sent by God were the only proofs Jesus gave John, and the only ones he gave us whereby to judge any one who claimed to be God's special messenger. These same fruits established the claims of his disciples as well.

As Jesus the Christ passed to and fro over the plain of Judea, preaching the Gospel of the kingdom, and healing the people of their diseased conditions, he thus established his claim to the Messiahship.

In the twelfth chapter of Matthew we read: *Then was brought unto him one possessed with a devil, blind, and dumb: and he healed him, insomuch that the blind and dumb both spake and saw. And all the people were amazed, and said, Is not this the son of David?* This infuriated the Pharisees and Scribes because they began to realize that he was thus establishing his claim to the Messiahship, as had been prophesied by Isaiah centuries before.

They not only deliberately and positively rejected Jesus Christ, the Saviour of the world, as the promised Messiah, but also the signs which God in His infinite wisdom, had decreed and ordained as the positive and unfailing proof of his Messiahship as well. This, however, did not satisfy their mad ambition to ruin him. They went much further in their wilful and evil determination to destroy Jesus Christ by deliberately and specifically accusing him of healing the sick, the lame, the deaf, the dumb, and the blind by the power of "Beelzebub, the prince of devils."

Jesus had patiently borne all they said against him personally, but when they thus maliciously and diabolically accused him of doing his great healing by the power of the evil one, he boldly stepped forth and uttered the most severe, most startling, and most solemn warning against men attributing the healing power of the Christ-cure to "Beelzebub, the prince of devils," that ever fell from the lips of the son of the Most High.

He said unto them: *Every kingdom divided against itself is brought to desolation; and every city or house divided against itself shall not stand: And if Satan cast out Satan, he is divided against himself; how shall then his kingdom stand? And if I by Beelzebub cast out devils, by whom do your children cast them out? therefore they shall be your judges. But if I cast out devils by the Spirit of God, then the kingdom of God is come unto you. . . . Wherefore I say unto you, All manner of sin and blasphemy shall be forgiven unto men: but the blasphemy against the Holy Ghost shall not be forgiven unto men. And whosoever speaketh a word against the Son of man, it shall be forgiven him: but whosoever speaketh against the Holy Ghost, it shall not be forgiven him, neither in this world, neither in the world to come.*

Again, in the case of the healing of the man born blind we have another example of how desperately the leaders of the people viewed the situation, and how determined they were to counteract these many proofs of his claim to the Messiahship which Jesus demonstrated on every hand. They tried to make the man healed of total blindness admit that Jesus Christ could not be of God, because he healed on the Sabbath Day. When this failed they tried to discredit the fact that the man had ever been blind; nor did this help them out of their dilemma. So they agreed that anyone who professed that Jesus was the Christ, should be put out of the synagogue. This frightened the young man's parents, but it did not deter the man who was healed from holding to and openly professing he had been healed of total blindness by the Saviour, and that never before had such a healing taken place among men.

In the face of all their opposition, Jesus the Christ moved steadily forward doing the works that established beyond a doubt, the fact that he was the real Messiah. This stirred the Pharisees and the chief priests to such a state of anger against Christ,— the Truth, that they finally crucified Jesus, thinking that in this way they would undo all his mighty works—the proof of his Messiahship—and annihilate his teachings, which were causing them so much trouble, and undermining their false concept of true worship. But this was impossible.

In less than sixty days after the crucifixion they had to face it again. On the day of Pentecost, when the multitude came together to see what had taken place—for the disciples had received the Holy

Ghost, and had come into this higher and clearer understanding of the Christ and of the Scriptures as well—Peter stood up before the very men who had crucified his Master, and plainly told them that he was their promised Messiah and that his blood was upon their hands. Moreover, that he had openly, and beyond all question, given them the undeniable signs which their own prophet Isaiah had said would be the very proof of his Messiahship, and which the Master had taught Peter and the other apostles, was the only indisputable proof or demonstration of the fact that the messenger was from God. *Ye men of Israel,* spoke Peter, *hear these words; Jesus of Nazareth, a man approved of God among you by miracles and wonders and signs, which God did by him in the midst of you, as ye yourselves also know: . . . ye have taken, and by wicked hands have crucified and slain: . . . Now when they heard this, they were pricked in their heart, and said unto Peter and to the rest of the Apostles, Men and brethren, what shall we do? Then Peter said unto them, Repent, and be baptized every one of you in the name of Jesus Christ for the remission of sins, and ye shall receive the gift of the Holy Ghost. For the promise is unto you, and to your children, and to all that are afar off, even as many as the Lord our God shall call. . . . Then they that gladly received his word were baptized: and the same day there were added unto them about three thousand souls.* Thus Peter, too, established for all time that men need no more or further proofs than those given by Jesus the Christ to identify his God-given mission, and of his being a messenger sent by God.

Did Mrs. Eddy, the Discoverer and Founder of Christian Science, produce these proofs? She certainly did. It was through her ability to heal the sick, the lame, the blind, the deaf, the mentally deranged, the drunkard, and the immoral man of his sins and sinful habits in Christ's way that she established herself beyond any doubt as God's messenger to this age. Not only did she produce these Christly proofs of her high calling, but she also proved that her teachings and writings were indeed God-inspired. For her students, and her students' students, as well as her textbook, have healed and are healing the sick and the sinful. These living epistles of what she has done, and is doing, for mankind through her teachings and writings are today numbered by hundreds of thousands.

That Mrs. Eddys' place in God's plan for the redemption of mankind is becoming clearer and more fully understood in the religious world today is certain. The evidence of this fact is fast accumulating on every hand. Men are beginning to realize as never before, the quality of the fruits of Christian Science in the form of the intelligence and high Christian character developed in her followers. This must be conceded as the best and highest proof of Mrs. Eddy's worth, and the correctness of her teachings. Not only are these results seen in America where her work originated, but also among all civilized people and nations of the earth.

Now who was Mrs. Eddy, the fruit of whose religious system called Christian Science I had tasted of, and through which I had been so wondrously healed? I soon learned that Mrs. Eddy was the Discoverer and Founder of Christian Science, and also the Author of its textbook, *Science and Health with Key to the Scriptures,* which is the only textbook on Christian Science.

In the study of this, her textbook, I learned that Christian Science was the rediscovery of the truth as taught by Jesus the Christ, revealing and setting forth the Principle underlying his teachings that conquered sin, disease, and death.

Notwithstanding all the good that was flowing into my life, and the better and higher understanding that I was gaining of God, man, and the Scriptures through the study of *Science and Health,* coupled with my deep desire to know the Truth, I failed to realize at the time the important fact that this was my dear heavenly Father's loving way of answering my unceasing prayer for a closer walk with Him, as well as His loving desire to equip me more thoroughly to preach His Gospel and carry out His command to heal the sick.

I was unable to see that every thing Mrs. Eddy taught was the Truth. The reason for this, I now realize, was due to the fact that I was much blinded with my old and false theological beliefs, and also that I was prejudiced against the Discoverer and Founder of Christian Science—the Author of its textbook. And why? Much because Mrs. Eddy was a woman, and not some great and world-renowned theologian. Had she been a theological professor, or a distinguished bishop in the Methodist Episcopal Church, I might have swallowed the textbook whole; but this would not, of course, have been a real acceptance of its teachings so long as it rested simply on some human personality, and it would have been but a short time before I would have fallen by the wayside.

Yet, here a comparatively unknown New England woman had boldly stepped forth and had presented to the world in a most convincing manner teachings, that, if accepted, would overthrow most of the old, theological views about God, Mind, Spirit, Christ, Truth, the Holy Ghost, science, man, angel, soul, body, heaven, hell, judgment, prayer, nature, cause and effect, as well as the machinations of evil. In fact, well nigh everything we had been taught was analyzed and laid bare, and its falsity shown by this new and undaunted exponent of the real teachings of Jesus Christ.

I felt that this was more than I could accept, and so long as I could not agree with all of her teachings, I concluded it would be best for me, for the time being, to work in my old field, utilizing what I could of the good I had received and was receiving through the study of her textbook.

I was in a receptive frame of mind, and the burden of all my prayers, as I have stated before, was that I might know God better, and be more fully equipped to do His work. It was some time before I saw clearly the absolute importance of seeing the Discoverer and Founder of Christian Science in the true light, and recognizing her place in the plan of redemption of mankind.

When this light broke in on my mind and consciousness, Christian Science unfolded to me rapidly, and it was a great and unceasing joy to see my false beliefs disappear, and to realize that at last I had come to see, understand, and demonstrate how the sick were healed in Jesus' way, and thus be able to carry out the whole of Christ's command to *Go ye into all the world, and preach the gospel to every creature. . . . And these signs shall follow them that believe; In my name shall they cast out devils; they shall speak with new tongues; They shall take up serpents; and if they drink any deadly thing, it shall not hurt them; they shall lay hands on the sick, and they shall recover* (Mark 16: 15-18).

CHAPTER III

s soon as I realized something of what Christian Science had done for me I sought at once to procure a copy of *Science and Health,* but the bookstores did not carry the volume in those days; neither were there any Christian Science Reading Rooms where I might purchase it. My practitioner, however, kindly assisted me, and sent to Boston for a copy; this required some time. In the meantime I secured a copy of one of Mrs. Eddy's earliest publications on Christian Science, a sermon entitled, "The People's Idea of God," which she had delivered in Boston, Massachusetts. I found "The People's Idea of God" very interesting and instructive. It was the first from Mrs. Eddy's pen I had ever read.

Just about this time our Presiding Elder came to La Crosse to hold our Quarterly Conference, and naturally the first subject we discussed was my wonderful healing through Christian Science, and what had brought it about. He was much interested and most grateful to God for my healing. He read this sermon by the Discoverer and Founder of Christian Science with deep interest, and was very complimentary in his remarks about its instructive message of Truth and Love.

As soon as my copy of *Science and Health* came I devoted much time to the study of its contents. I found, however, the teachings so divergent and foreign to my old orthodox theological views that I hesitated in accepting everything Mrs. Eddy had written.

But her teachings on the subject of healing the sick interested me deeply, and I am grateful to God, that I grasped the Principle of Christian Science healing quickly. It proved a great blessing to me in every way, and in the course of time led me into a fuller understanding of Mrs. Eddy's teachings.

In September, 1886—about two months following my healing—I was sent to a church in Minneapolis, Minnesota. It was a large and difficult field, but I was not daunted, and joyfully accepted the appointment. The work prospered along better and higher lines of spiritual development as I made use of the knowledge I had of Christian Science.

My predecessor was unable to take a charge that year on account of ill-health. He was, it was said, in the last stages of tuberculosis, and I was asked by some of the ministers in the Conference to take him to a Christian Science practitioner to see if he could be healed as I had been. Think of it! Methodist ministers were asking me to take another Methodist minister to a Christian Science practitioner! And the reason for this? They knew little or nothing of Christian Science and its teachings; but they did know it to be a fact that I had been wonderfully healed through its ministry. Later on, however, things radically changed, and some of them became suspicious of Christian Science and of those who followed its teachings.

Arriving in my new field of labor, I made it my first duty to take the above-mentioned minister to a practitioner. He was glad to go, and at first seemed to respond to the treatment. Finally he began to ask questions concerning the teachings of Mrs. Eddy, and I judged from all he said, that perhaps the practitioner, in her eagerness to help him, gave him more than he could assimilate in so short a time, whereas she should have led him gently along until he had gained a little understanding of Christian Science. The result was that he found Christian Science so at variance with his orthodox views that in the mental upheaval produced he turned away from it before he was fully healed.

This was a lesson to me, and it taught me to be more careful in dealing with a beginner in Christian Science; especially if the beginner were a minister or a physician, I have found that too great care cannot be exercised in a case of this kind. One must wait until God has prepared the soil.

In the parable of the sower, the Master beautifully illustrates this important fact. He said, *When any one heareth the word of the kingdom, and understandeth it not, then cometh the wicked one, and catcheth away that which was sown in his heart . . . But he that received seed into the good ground is he that heareth the word, and understandeth it; which also beareth fruit, and bringeth forth, some an hundred fold, some sixty, some thirty* (Matt. 13:19-23).

When the spirit of God has been given an opportunity to move upon the waters of mortal mind, and has prepared it for the reception of the Truth, it will be found that these men who as a general thing are well versed in their respective callings, become most willing disciples, and will gladly learn their lessons all over again—commence anew, as it were.

While at first I was unable to accept all of the teachings of Mrs. Eddy, I did get the understanding of how to heal the sick. However, there developed such bitter opposition in the churches—

especially in the Methodist Church—against Christian Science after Dr. James M. Buckley had written a long article in one of the best magazines derogatory to Mrs. Eddy and what he thought was Christian Science, that it was no longer safe for anyone to say or do much in its favor if he wanted to stand well in the denomination.

The ministers no longer came to me requesting I take some sick brother to a practitioner for healing. Instead, they began to question if I had not been led into a "dangerous heresy" which some claimed was neither Christian nor scientific. Some of the brethren, though, came and talked with me concerning Christian Science in order to draw me out—in like manner as did the Pharisees with Jesus, a description of which is portrayed in the twenty-second chapter of Matthew: *Then went the Pharisees, and took counsel how they might entangle him in his talk. And they sent out unto him their disciples with the Herodians, saying, Master, we know that thou art true, and teachest the way of God in truth, neither carest thou for any man: for thou regardest not the person of men. Tell us therefore, What thinkest thou? Is it lawful to give tribute unto Caesar, or not? But Jesus perceived their wickedness, and said, Why tempt ye me, ye hypocrites? Shew me the tribute money. And they brought unto him a penny. And he saith unto*

them, Whose is this image and superscription?
They say unto him, Caesar's. Then saith he unto
them, Render therefore unto Caesar the things
which are Caesar's; and unto God the things that
are God's. When they had heard these words, they
marvelled, and left him, and went their way.

I recall that one of the leading ministers in the
Conference, who was widely known for his ex-
treme orthodox views on nearly every religious
subject, asked me one day if I believed in a personal devil. When I frankly told him I did not,
he fairly gasped for breath. For he believed just
as faithfully in a personal devil as he did in God.
The dear man believed himself to be much opposed to Mrs. Eddy and her teachings for years;
but about twenty years later, he began to think
better of Christian Science and those who believed
in it. He developed a case of cancer and suffered
untold agony for months. Finally he was told by
his many doctors that there was no hope for him,
and when he realized that he had but a few hours
to live, he wired a Christian Science practitioner
for help. But the practitioner arrived too late—
just as he was passing out. It was a joy, however,
to me, to hear he had softened a little towards
Christian Science, and was at last reaching out
for its healing power.

During the early pioneer days of Christian Science, the public press was quite hostile towards Mrs. Eddy and her teachings, and frequently published bitter attacks on its Leader and the cause of Christian Science. I found that some of the ministers in my Conference became very much contaminated by these false reports. There were some exceptions, and I was able to interest these to the extent that they took up the reading of the textbook, some even taking treatment. After one of these friends was healed in Christian Science he became a faithful student, finally taking his stand for Christian Science, and resigning from the Methodist Episcopal Church and ministry. He is now a successful practitioner.

As a general thing, the ministers were strongly opposed to Christian Science, and soon began to watch me to see if I were really sound in the Methodist doctrine. I well remember an experience at a camp-meeting I attended. The Presiding Elder and I were entertained in the same home. He was very friendly towards Christian Science, and we often had good talks together on the subject. One evening he told me how the "brethren" were watching me, and hunting for heresy. He advised me to be a little more discreet, and not talk too freely about Christian Science. He frankly told me he did not want me to jeopardize my standing in the church, nor do anything which would in any way curtail my usefulness as a Methodist minister, especially as long as I could not conscientiously accept all the teachings of Mrs. Eddy. In our talks on Christian Science I made it plain to him that while I found much good in the writings of Mrs. Eddy, I was unable to accept all her teachings. He said, "Personally I do not find anything in what you have explained to me concerning Christian Science, or what I have read in Mrs. Eddy's book, to which I can take exception. As you are aware, I have a very limited knowledge on the subject, so I cannot say any more; you should move slowly until you see your way more clearly." I told him I had to be true to my highest understanding, but I would keep his kindly suggestion in mind.

The next day was my turn to preach. My text was taken from Acts, 1:8: *But ye shall receive power, after that the Holy Ghost is come upon you: and ye shall be witnesses unto me both in Jerusalem, and in all Judea, and in Samaria, and unto the uttermost part of the earth.* We had what the Methodists call "a good time." Many came to me after the service and thanked me kindly for the sermon. Among those extending their compliments was an elderly minister, who told me what a wonderful sermon it was, and how much good it had brought him. Then he added, "But what did you mean?" I smiled and replied, "I meant just what I said." He looked a bit puzzled and then said, "Oh! I did not know but that you had another meaning in mind." He was evidently on a hunting expedition for heresy.

I shall ever be grateful to God for the many blessed experiences I had during these early years of my interest in Christian Science, as it gave me many opportunities to present to some of my friends the healing power of Christian Science; and, too, I am now aware that the good seed planted bore fruit.

By the understanding that had come to me through the study of the textbook of Christian Science, I was enabled to heal the sick, and thus care for the physical needs of my family for years before I entered the active Christian Science work. Consequently most of our children grew up without even knowing the taste of medicine. We realize today we cannot be too deeply grateful to God that we were granted the great privilege of teaching the children the blessings of the Christ-cure—Christian Science, as one of their earliest and most important lessons, thereby eliminating as much as possible their holding to any false beliefs or theories concerning sin, disease, and death as a reality.

The good seed sown in the fertile soil of the child's mind is never lost, and it is most gratifying to us today to see how this transforming truth bears its fruitage, enabling them to successfully apply the Principle of Christian Science to their daily problems in life, and help others as well.

I was unable to do much outside of my own family, except in a quiet way, on account of the strong prejudice in the church against divine Science; nevertheless I had some wonderful demonstrations of the power of God to heal the sick as well as the sinning.

I well remember calling one evening on a family to see their little son who was very ill. When I arrived the doctor had just left, and the father told me the physician had given the boy up, advising them he could not live through the night; furthermore it would be useless to call him again, as everything had been done for the child that could be done. He said he would call in the morning on his way to see other patients, and bring the boy's death certificate.

When the sorrowing parent told me all this, I said to myself, "Come what may, I will tell these good people what had healed me." I did so. They forthwith appealed to me to do something for their child. I treated him in Christian Science and he was completely healed in one treatment. When the doctor arrived with the boy's "death certificate" the following morning, he found the lad well, and up and dressed.

Another instance which I recall, was that of a neighbor of ours who was dying with pneumonia. The doctor had given him up, and I was asked to do what I could for him. I treated him, and he also was beautifully healed through this blessed Truth of Christian Science.

There were only a very few Christian Scientists in Minneapolis when I lived there, and they had no church. Now there are six large and prosperous churches in that beautiful city.

From Minneapolis I was transferred to a church in Chicago, Illinois. The good Lord continued to bless my efforts and large numbers of people were beautifully converted to God in every church I served. I noticed this, however, that the more closely I adhered to Mrs. Eddy's interpretation of the Scriptures, the greater success I had. It fed the people with the "bread of heaven" as nothing else could. When I was stationed in Chicago, the Christian Scientists had but one church. Today they have eighteen large and beautiful churches. I was allowed to remain in Chicago but one year, as our Bishop wanted me for a church in Racine, Wisconsin.

An amusing little incident occurred the day before I left for Conference. The secretary of our Church said to me in a pleasant way, "Brother Simonsen, do you know we have been watching you the whole year?" I laughed and replied, "Yes, I suppose so. It would be the natural thing for a church to do; but did you find anything in my preaching or teaching that was not in accordance with the teachings of Christ?" "No," he answered, "if we had, you no doubt would have heard from us, for we were told by two of our former pastors that you were interested in Christian Science, and might not be sound in Methodism." These two good brethren tried the same tactics in Racine, and again in Brooklyn, but without effect. I was sorry though, to see the manifestation of such a spirit.

CHAPTER IV

The Climax

N Racine, Wisconsin, I found a most delightful and appreciative church to serve. My pastorate there was also marked not only by a large increase in membership, but also in the spiritual unfoldment of the people. I was also enabled to do much valuable work in that city in the cause of temperance, as had been my good fortune to do in every city where I had been permitted to preach the Gospel of Christ.

While in Racine, both my eldest son and I were stricken with a severe attack of scarlet fever. We were beautifully healed through Christian Science, and suffered no after effects.

From Racine I was transferred, in 1892, to the New York East Conference, and stationed in Brooklyn, New York. Here I remained for many years, and enjoyed the most successful pastorate in my whole career as a Methodist minister.

It was in Brooklyn that I experienced the great climax of my life. I was happy and successful in my church work, but a great conflict was going on in my own mind as to whether Christian Science were really the Truth or not. If it were the Truth I wanted it, and I would gladly commend it to my people; and especially did I desire to tell the sick of its healing power. If it were not the Truth, could I send my people into something I could not myself accept? Yet when visiting the sick, it was most heartrending to sit by the bedside of a dying mother or father whose families needed them so much, and not be free to tell them of the Truth which had healed me when I was given up to die by every physician that examined me. I knew, though, it would destroy my usefulness as a Methodist minister if I did; and so long as I felt I was not ready to take my stand and enter the Christian Science fold, I deemed it only prudent to bide my time.

I therefore set myself to the task and did as Jesus advised one to do, who contemplated building "a tower," to see if I had sufficient understanding not only to begin to build the tower, but to complete it as well. For he said: *For which of you, intending to build a tower, sitteth not down first, and counteth the cost, whether he have sufficient to finish it? Lest haply, after he hath laid the*

*foundation, and is not able to finish it, all that be-
hold it begin to mock him, saying, This man began
to build, and was not able to finish* (Luke
14:28-30). When I realized that I did not have
this understanding, I concluded to *wait for the
promise of the Father* (Acts 1:4).

About this time, when I was going through
this mental conflict, one of our children was taken
ill with a claim which I was seemingly unable to
handle. Then the question arose: should we call
for Christian Science help? After going into the
matter carefully with my good wife, we decided to
let an M.D.—a specialist—try his hand at the case
first. If he did not succeed in a reasonable time,
we would then feel free to turn to Christian Science.

This we did, but the doctor failed. We then
turned to Christian Science. Our first practitioner
worked faithfully, but did not seem to reach the
case either. Then a teacher in Christian Science,
who afterwards became my primary teacher, suggested we try another practitioner; and also com-
municated with her by telephone.

This good lady said she would like to have a
talk with me before she could decide to take the
case. I consented, and we had a most interesting
interview. She asked me some searching questions.
The first one was, "Why do you, a minister of

Jesus Christ, come to me, a Christian Scientist, for help for your child?" I told her of my own healing, and that I no longer had faith in *Materia Medica* so thought best to turn to Christian Science.

Then she asked me, "Don't you, as a minister of the gospel of Christ, heal the sick?" I told her I was deeply interested in the subject, but that I really did not know anything about the Principle of the Christ healing, except what I had learned through Christian Science, but that evidently I did not have sufficient understanding to heal this case. Then she asked me, "Does not your church heal the sick?" I had to confess to her that it did not. Then she put this searching question to me, "Can you expect God to heal your child in Christian Science when you are not willing to openly acknowledge what He has done for you through Christian Science?" I am deeply grateful to God for these direct questions which did much to awaken me to the true situation confronting me.

Finally the practitioner said she would take the case if I would place myself under her treatment also, "For," she said, "by getting your thought straightened out, it would facilitate the healing of your child." This, I found afterward, was a cardinal point, in treating children's cases. I consented.

The good lady was very kind, patient, and painstaking in trying to lead me out of my old ideas into Christian Science. She gave me a great deal of her time, and we had many helpful discussions on Christian Science.

As I progressed in my understanding of the teachings of Mrs. Eddy, I became more and more awakened to the fact that if I found her teachings to be the Truth, it would take me, root and branch, out of the Methodist Church and its ministry; and I told the practitioner so. To this she calmly replied, "What of that?" I answered with emphasis, "The 'What of that' means a great deal to me in more ways than one; for instance, the question of supply. If I took this step I would cut myself off from all income, and not only that, but it would at the same time deprive my wife and seven children of the aid they would be entitled to from our Minister's Aid Society in the event I passed on." I confessed to her that it looked like a momentous problem, and especially as I had not been able to lay aside a dollar. To this she deliberately enquired, "Do you not think God is just as able to support you and yours in Christian Science as He is in Methodism?" I said, "Yes, I suppose He is; but the question is, have I sufficient faith and understanding to make this demonstration?" She was unable, however, to point to a single individual who had so large a family to care for as I had, who had successfully made such a demonstration; neither did I know of any who had.

Nevertheless I did not let this or any other of the many serious problems which confronted me, and crowded my mind, delay me any longer in my search for the Truth. I had arrived at the point in my experience when I no longer was seeking Christian Science—The "Pearl of great price,"—and the understanding of its Principle simply for what it could do for my child physically, but I was seeking it because I believed it to be the Truth.

Finally I decided to take class-instruction. Mrs. Simonsen and I applied to one of Mrs. Eddy's personal and loyal students for admission to her next class. The teacher said she would not decide my case before she had consulted Mrs. Eddy, as I was still actively engaged in the Methodist ministry. Mrs. Eddy replied, "Yes, take Mr. Simonsen, but handle him without gloves." I am grateful to say, she did. We had a most interesting class. Among the members were a lawyer, a doctor, and myself, a clergyman, who kept the teacher busy answering all sorts of important questions pertaining to Christian Science.

It was indeed a most wonderful and helpful experience to me. During the class I was healed of my old theological beliefs, and was led to see and understand clearly that Mrs. Eddy's teachings were the teachings of Jesus Christ. I was not only able to see, but to understand and realize beyond all doubt, that the same Principle which heals sin, heals sickness as well. When this was clear to me I was leagues on the way in healing the sick; for I demonstrated in any number of cases that God heals all kinds of sin. I saw, too, and understood with equal clarity, that the same Principle which heals all manner of sin and sickness, also heals all manner of diseased financial and business conditions as well. Yes, in short it heals with equal certainty all erroneous conditions; for *the leaves of the tree* (the God Principle) *were for the healing of the nations* (Rev. 22:2).

When I entered the class there were three questions of paramount importance to be answered to satisfy my mind. The first and foremost: "Were the teachings of Christian Science the teachings of Jesus Christ?" Second: "Would Christian Science meet my financial conditions, and make it clear to my understanding how God could and would take care of me and mine?" And finally, "Could I meet the ridicule and persecution which would naturally follow a step of this kind?" Christian Science was not as popular then as it is today. I found that when the first and second questions were fully answered and thoroughly settled, the third question did not seem to bother me at all.

The climax was reached when I realized that there was only one thing for me to do as an honest man, and that was to take my stand for Christian Science. I could not stand in the Methodist Pulpit, preaching the Methodist doctrines, and be a Christian Scientist at heart; neither could I stand in a Methodist pulpit and preach Christian Science, for this would not be tolerated by the authorities of the church. Consequently there was only one thing for me to do, and that was for me to resign from the Methodist Episcopal Church and its ministry.

Just as Mrs. Simonsen and I were going through class, my brother, who was a minister and the president of a theological seminary in the Middle West, came and visited with us while he was attending a meeting in New York City of the Missionary Board of the Methodist Church, of which he was a member. When he was informed I was taking class-instruction in Christian Science, he became much disturbed, and warned me to have nothing to do with it. I may add, he was the first person to speak to me about Christian Science. Some days later we had a good heart-to-heart talk on the subject, and when he fully realized I was in earnest, and sincerely conscientious in the matter, he softened up considerably, saying, "I do not understand Christian Science, I cannot make much out of it; but this one thing I will say, that ever since you came in touch with it, you have been able to do two or three men's work in every charge you have served; and every church you have ministered unto would be only too glad to have you come back to them." I thanked him for the compliment.

The topic became of greater interest to him, and he desired to know what the Christian Science Church could offer me in the way of a position; for, he said, "You know, it is customary in other denominations, when a minister leaves one denomination to join another, a berth is provided for him." I replied, "In Christian Science things are different. A man comes into Christian Science because he sees and realizes that it is the Truth, and he makes his own demonstration as far as place and work are concerned." He thought of it as a most unheard-of situation.

The foregoing conversation must have worried him quite a little; for a few days later, as we were having lunch together in New York City, just before he took the train to return home, we resumed discussing my proposed step. He suddenly turned to me and asked, "How do you intend to support your large family?" I replied, "God will provide for us." He looked startled and said, "You must be losing your mind." "No," I said, "I am not, I am coming into my right mind."

He looked serious, and gravely enquired, "What do you think our good father would say if he were here and knew you were contemplating leaving the Methodist Church and ministry for Christian Science?" To this I replied: "I do not think Father would object if he knew I was conscientious, and had found that Christian Science had given me not only a higher and better understanding of God, the Scriptures, and man, but it had enabled me to carry out Christ's command to go and heal the sick, as well as preach the Gospel. You know the time came in Father's life when he saw that the teachings of the Methodist Church were higher and better than those of the Lutheran Church and when this light came to him he resigned and joined the first named denomination." "Yes," he rejoined, "that is true; but take your time, brother, and be not in a hurry to take so important a step." I assured him I was not acting in haste, but had prayerfully and conscientiously considered the subject for a longer period of time than St. Paul had spent in Arabia before he ventured to go up to Jerusalem.

During the weeks and months that preceded

the writing of my resignation, I had a hard battle. At times it seemed "as dark as Egypt." Error surged about me like a wild storm in the dead of night. The dark billows of fear and evil forebodings as to my future, tried their best to engulf my little bark; but I clung persistently and steadfastly to my dear heavenly Father, who carried me safely over it all. In the midst of these momentous days I had some wonderful experiences which showed me beyond all doubt that He was leading me step by step. For instance:

I asked my assistant Pastor to preach for me one Sunday morning, and I slipped away to attend a Christian Science service. I started bright and early so as to get away before my people would begin to come to church. We lived in the parsonage which was next door to the church. At the first stop after I boarded the street car, who should enter but the wife of our organist. I knew she was slightly interested in Christian Science, and the thought came to me that in all probability she also was going to this same church. Then the suggestion came to me to change my course, go over to New York City, and attend one of the Christian Science Churches there; for if the good lady should see me in the church in Brooklyn, she would undoubtedly tell her husband, he in turn tell the choir, and it would not be long before the entire church would know it; then there would be trouble ahead.

I stood my ground, and said to myself, "I have dodged this question long enough. I will go where I set out to go, come what may." It so happened that we had to change cars to reach the church. When I got off, my friend alighted also and said, "Good morning, Pastor; seems to me you are straying from home." I answered by asking if she were not also straying from her accustomed place of worship. She admitted it, and added, she was going down on the De Kalb Avenue car-line—the one I had to take to reach the Christian Science Church. Then we changed the subject and talked about the weather.

In due time the car came along and we boarded it. We had not ridden long before the car stopped and some ladies entered, one greeting me very cordially. Presently my friend, in an undertone, asked me if I knew her, and then said, "She is a Christian Science practitioner." I replied, "Yes, I know it, and I am going to attend the Christian Science Church this morning." She looked surprised and said, "You are? Well, I am going there too; but I was ashamed to tell you so." We both enjoyed the service, and at the close were heartily greeted; and I was deeply impressed by the love and happiness expressed in the faces of the large congregation.

On our way back to the trolley car my friend said to me, "Mr. Simonsen, are you greatly interested in Christian Science?" I informed her I was looking into it. Then again on the street car she turned to me and said, "Pastor, I believe you are deeply interested in Christian Science; and it comes to me that some day you will leave the Methodist ministry, and go into Christian Science work." I tried to act surprised, and asked her why she thought so. She replied, "Because you are so deeply interested in the subject." I turned the conversation to something else as soon as I could, for it was rather an embarrassing subject for me to discuss just then. My mind was occupied with little else, and at the same time, I was not fully prepared to step into the open.

As we were nearing home I looked at my watch and realized that I might meet my own people coming out of church, for our service was longer than the Christian Science service. At once fear began to assert itself. This would never do, I thought; for of course they would be interested to know where their pastor had preached, or had attended service; and what should I say? Then the suggestion came to me to get off one block this side, walk around and enter the parsonage from the other street, thus avoiding meeting them, or at least most of them. But I said, "No, I will not do that; I will face the music."

Just then I recalled a lady, a member of my congregation, who was ill with quick consumption. She lived a few doors off from the street I was traveling on. This seemed a fine way to escape my people; so I left the car, and went to call on this lady. When I arrived, I found that they had a number of doctors—experts on consumption—and they all pronounced her case fatal. They said she could live but three weeks, and that they could not move her to a hospital, for the shock would cause instant death. I realized I must take my stand after all; so I told them about my wonderful healing through Christian Science, and what I knew it could do for them. Suddenly the lady suffered a severe hemorrhage. The husband appealed to me to do what I could for her, for I had also told them about some of the cases of healing, the result of my work.

The first thing I found myself doing was to drop on my knees and begin to implore God to heal her. But I was at once arrested by "a still small voice," which said to me "Why do you ask God to be God? Why do you not get up and treat the lady? You know enough about the blessed Truth to heal her." I stopped my pleading at once,

arose and sat down, and treated her. The hemorrhage stopped immediately; she rested easy and
fell asleep. I left them and neither saw nor heard
from them again before the following Sunday when
they walked briskly into my church. I was in the
pulpit at the time, and I was almost overcome by
what I saw. To think that I really had the understanding to heal a case of quick consumption in
one treatment seemed almost too good to be true.
After the service I went directly to this couple, and
I said to the good lady, "How is this?" She immediately replied, "Why Mr. Simonsen, I am perfectly well," and indeed she looked the picture of
health.

This gave me fresh courage, and then came
the thought that I ought to help a poor lady—a
member of our church—who was in the Kings
County Hospital for the Insane, and who had been
confined in different institutions for six years. The
doctors had said she could not be healed.

I visited her once, and continued treating her
each day thereafter for a period of three weeks.
Then I wrote the Superintendent and enquired
about her. The doctor replied immediately, stating
she was perfectly well and normal, and if I would
come out there and sign papers to the effect that
I would be responsible for her conduct and board
for thirty days, I could take her out any time. I

lost no time, but went out on an early train the next morning and brought her home with me. She has been well and happy ever since.

Some years later, my brother, who had felt so humiliated at the stand I had taken for Christian Science, visited my old church, and after the service this lady met him and told him what I had done for her through Christian Science. He wrote me afterwards, "Well, if you can do these things, brother, I have nothing more to say."

These beautiful healings proved a great blessing to me just at this time when I was making up my mind to take this important step of leaving all for Christian Science. I shall ever thank God for them, for they were clear proofs of the truth of Mrs. Eddy's teachings.

Shortly before Thanksgiving, I came to the point where I both saw and realized beyond the shadow of a doubt, that Christian Science was the Truth and nothing but the Truth, *Whereupon, . . . I was not disobedient unto the heavenly vision.* but at once took my stand for Science.

On the morning of the day before Thanksgiving, I told my dear wife that I was going to write my resignation from the Methodist Episcopal Church and ministry; and that I must not be disturbed on any account, unless there was a fire in the house, or some one was dying and wanted to see me. Neither were they to call me for luncheon; I would come when I was hungry. In my seclusion I started to write my resignation, but the longer I struggled the darker it grew, until about three-thirty o'clock in the afternoon, when still laboring wearily to formulate my resignation, I heard a voice which said to me, "Why are you taking this step anyway?" It awakened me to such an extent that I picked up some paper and a pencil, and arising, I took a seat in a large armchair and commenced to jot down why I was taking this step. I found myself enumerating the things Christian Science had done for me and mine, and what it had brought to me in the line of a better, higher, and clearer understanding of God and man, of God's relationship to man, of man's relationship to God, and man's relationship to man. This acted like a heroic treatment, and broke the mesmeric spell that seemingly gripped me and darkened my mind for a bit. I returned to my desk and wrote my resignation without any further trouble. It proved to be God-inspired, for many people who later read it in the public press were led into Christian Science through reading it.

That same evening we had our Quarterly Conference. After the routine business was taken care of, and the usual question by the Presiding Elder was asked, "Is there any further business?" I told him I had a communication to the Conference which I would ask the Secretary to read. Thereupon I handed in my resignation, and asked to be excused from the Conference. The Doctor said as I was leaving, **"You are coming back,** are you not, Brother Simonsen?" I said, "No, I have nothing further to do here," and walked out.

The step I had taken was a complete surprise to the Conference, and after reading my resignation the Presiding Elder asked the Board, "How long has this been going on?" They all said it was news to them, except the Secretary of the Conference, who said he knew I had been healed through Christian Science; also that I had recently told him I was interested in the subject, and was making a thorough investigation of its teachings; but aside from that, he had no idea I was contemplating such a step as this.

They discussed the case, and what had better be done in the matter, until well nigh midnight, the Elder requesting the members of the Board not to mention the matter to any one for the present. He said that he would take it up with the Bishop, and then would call on me to see if I would not reconsider and withdraw my resignation.

The following day was Thanksgiving, the last in the old century, and I made an early call on the

Secretary of the Board to enquire what had been done regarding my resignation. When he entered the room where I was seated, his face wore a long-drawn-out expression, and he was most serious. His greeting was, "Oh, Pastor, you have made the mistake of your life." I immediately denied this, stating also that I had taken this step only after a prayerful and painstaking investigation of Christian Science, and of what it would mean, not only to me and mine, but also to the Cause. I was sure of my ground, and I knew and realized clearly that I had done the right and only thing an honest and conscientious man could do after he had become convinced that Christian Science was in accordance with the teachings of Jesus Christ.

He tried in various ways to get me to see that it would be wise and best for me to reconsider my resignation, and withdraw it. He also begged me to let the matter rest for a time at least, and remain with them as they needed me. I told him frankly that I had been "between the bark and tree" long enough. I had "crossed the Rubicon," had "burned the bridges behind me," and the question was settled for all time.

Error seemed to unleash itself; for on my return to the parsonage, just as I was putting the latchkey in the door, I heard something falling down stairs.

When I opened the door, I found one of our little boys lying in a heap at the foot of the stairs, his face as white as a sheet. He and his brother had been standing at the second story window watching for my return, and when they saw me coming toward the steps, they had rushed into the hall and down the stairs to open the door for me. The younger boy running ahead, tripped at the top of the long flight of stairs and fell the whole length, seemingly breaking his arm just below the elbow. I picked him up in my arms and in doing so, felt impelled to pull his arm out straight, which I did. At once he screamed with pain, and aroused the entire family. I took him into the parlor while Mrs. Simonsen and the other children withdrew. There I sat down and treated him.

No sooner had I started to work for the boy than the suggestion came to me, "You had better send for a doctor to set the arm." Then error argued that Mrs. Eddy had said in *Science and Health,* one could have a doctor set the bone, and then care for the case in Christian Science.

I realized that would look bad to have to call in one of the medical fraternity the very next day after I had resigned from the Methodist Episcopal Church and ministry, because Christian Science had done and would do so much for me. "No," I said resolutely, "that will never do; God will have to care for the boy. I will trust Him, come what may." I went about my work for the child, and he soon quieted down, finally falling asleep.

I found, however, that the case needed more attention than I was able to give it that morning as I was busy getting ready to deliver a lecture the same evening; so I called in a practitioner and the boy was beautifully healed.

I was indeed grateful to God that the case was met in Christian Science. If I had called a doctor, it would no doubt have been a friend of mine, who a few months later, I recall, delivered a lecture against what he said was Christian Science. Doubtless he would have made good use of this instance had I called him in to attend my child. God, in His goodness, protected me and the Cause, and gave me further proof that He never forsakes us in the time of need.

The Presiding Elder called to see me the day after Thanksgiving. About the first thing he said was, "Brother Simonsen, you pretty nearly took our breath away Wednesday night when you handed in your resignation. Do you really mean to leave us? Will you not reconsider your step?" I said, "No, I will not reconsider it. It is final." "Well," he said, with much feeling, "I wish you had come to me and confided in me; I would have been glad to have labored with you and prayed for you." I thanked him, and candidly told him that I did not feel I could turn to him or any other human being in this crisis. It was a question wholly between God and myself.

He enquired when I wished my resignation to take effect, and I answered, "Just as soon as you can find another man to take the pulpit." We agreed that it should take effect on December 31st, 1900.

At his request, I named one or two ministers who, I thought, might be suitable for my old pulpit, and he selected one of them. He was very kind and complimentary about the work I had performed among them, saying, "I begrudge Christian Science a man of your ability." As he bade me good-bye, he said, "Brother Simonsen, I feel exceedingly sorry for you." I assured him he need not feel that way about it, for I was perfectly happy in my choice, and rejoiced in the glorious light and sense of freedom which had come to me through Christian Science, as well as for the practicable and demonstrable understanding of the Truth that was mine.

My elder brother, who had recently visited us, was not home many days before he received a copy of my resignation. It seemed to upset him very much, for he wrote me quite a letter in reply, and told me, among other things, how I had not only disgraced myself, but the entire family as well. When my eldest brother learned of the step I had taken, he wrote he had worried so much about me and my family that he could not sleep for three days and nights. One of my sisters said to me after a while, that she thought at first I had gone to the evil one and would be lost. She, however, was the first of my family to come into Christian Science.

At the next and last monthly meeting of our Church Board, the officials wanted to know why I had taken this step. I told them much of what I am relating here, and every man among them became interested. They said, "Brother Simonsen, we want you to stay and preach the Gospel to us in this new light; we need this kind of preaching." I told them that this was, I knew, just what they needed, and were hungering for; but that I would not be permitted to stand in their pulpit long, and preach the Gospel in the light of Christian Science, after the authorities of the church found out my views. However, if they would read *Science and Health,* by Mrs. Eddy, and study it as I had, they too would get this blessed understanding and realization of God and man. They were most kind to me. They knew I had to move, and wanted to know if I had found a house. I told them I had not; whereupon they very lovingly urged me to accept the free use of the parsonage for three months. I thanked them deeply for this kind and generous offer, but I told them I could not accept it; my successor would need it. I must find my new home, and get settled in my new line of work as quickly as possible.

The four or five Sundays that intervened between my resignation and the first of January were most interesting and far-reaching in their effects. The people just crowded the church to hear this blessed message of Truth and Love that I was permitted to bring to them during the closing hours of my ministry in the Methodist Church. It was indeed refreshing to me, for it was also an added proof that Mrs. Eddy's interpretation of the Scriptures was correct. Some of the good people enquired of the Secretary of the church, and said, "How is it that Mr. Simonsen preaches so differently, and with greater power than ever before?" He replied, "Mr. Simonsen feels perfectly free now and unhampered, and is preaching the Gospel according to his new-found understanding of the teachings of the Master." They expressed the wish that I would remain with them and continue this line of interpretation of the Scriptures, it being so satisfying and helpful to them.

I stepped out of the Methodist pulpit without one dollar to my name; in fact, I was in debt. Mrs. Simonsen had three or four hundred dollars which she generously placed at my disposal; and while we were in the midst of packing our goods preparatory to moving, some of the old church members gave us a surprise, and on their departure left a purse.

There were nine of us to be supported—Mrs. Simonsen, our seven small children, and myself. Until now we had been accustomed to finding a large and well furnished parsonage ready for our occupancy wherever we were sent. Now all this was changed. We had to go out and find our own home and furnish it throughout for our family. As I said before, there were nine to be fed, clothed, and kept warm, nine pair of feet to be hosed and shod: and if each were to have an extra pair, it would mean eighteen pair. An extra hat, as well as an extra suit of clothes for Sunday meant the purchase of eighteen hats and eighteen suits, and other needful things in like proportion.

It was most fortunate that Mrs. Simonsen and I were one in coming into Christian Science, as we have been in all our experiences. We had come right along together in Science from the first, going hand in hand every step of the way, just as we had done in everything since the day her good father had introduced me to his beautiful daughter, in their lovely home at Summit Corners, near Oconomowoc, Wisconsin.

I am deeply grateful to God to be able to say that our love has never waned in the least during all these forty-nine years, forty-four of which we have spent in a most happy married life. Perfect confidence in, love and tenderness for each other, as well as unselfishly seeking each other's happiness, has been our lot all these blessed years.

Mrs. Simonsen is the most devoted, capable, and loving wife and tender mother that any man could ask for. She is always well, strong and happy, radiant with sunshine and good cheer. She has a clear understanding of Christian Science and her healing work is most beautiful. Mrs. Simonsen was always in complete sympathy with every move I made. How fortunate, too, that we had been cautious and had taken the time to gain a sufficient understanding of Christian Science, and how to apply its Principle to the many serious, difficult, and trying problems we had to meet from day to day.

I shall ever be grateful that I waited on God until the fuller understanding of Christian Science came to me, before I took this far-reaching step. By taking my time and getting ready, I was able when I did embark, to weather the many storms that have surged with untold fury about me. Had I not exercised precaution, I do not know but that I, too, might have made shipwreck of my career in Christian Science as some other ministers have done.

I recall one instance that occurred some time after I had come into Science. A minister who had become interested in Christian Science, called to consult me in regard to his leaving his church and the ministry to go into Christian Science. After we had carefully gone over his case, fully analyzed each detail, he wanted to know if I thought he was fully prepared to take a step so vital and one so far-reaching in its effect. I candidly told him that it did not seem so to me, because it was plainly evident that he did not have sufficient understanding of Christian Science, and how to apply its Principle, at that time to make such an important move. Then, too, his wife was not in full sympathy with him, neither did he have any funds to support his family, nor the understanding of demonstrating substance, and how to protect himself and family against the many subtle forms of evil which were liable to strike at him.

His subsequent experience proved I was correct. He resigned from his church a few days after our talk and went into Christian Science; but I am sorry to have to record, that it was not long before he was compelled to retrace his steps, and return to his old church to resume his pulpit. He had failed to make good in the step he had taken because he did not have the necessary understanding to "build his tower."

It is plain to me that a minister who is deeply steeped in false theological beliefs, needs to be well rooted and grounded in his understanding of Christian Science in order to be able to successfully apply its Principle to the many problems which naturally would confront him from time to time. My experience has taught me that a layman cannot fully understand or realize all it means for a clergyman to take this step and hold it successfully after he has once taken it, any more than could the Jews, as for example, understand and realize what it meant to Saul of Tarsus, and what he had to meet, when he stepped out of the ranks of Judaism to boldly take his stand for Jesus Christ, to preach and practice Christianity throughout the then known world.

CHAPTER V

THE IMPORTANT STEP

 PREACHED my final sermon on the last night of the old century. The next day I stepped into the active healing work in Christian Science. After the service that night a majority of the congregation came forward to say good-bye. Many of them expressed their deep appreciation of what I had done for them in leading them into a new life, and for the spiritual enfoldment which had come to them through my ministry. Some, however, kindly told me that I had evidently missed my way and was fast headed for perdition. I denied this, and assured them that I never stood more securely on the Rock of Truth.

I shall long remember the peculiar feeling which came to me the next day—New Year's Day— as we sat down to our first dinner after I had resigned from the Methodist Episcopal Church and Ministry; had preached my last sermon, and had freely and deliberately given up all visible income. Mrs. Simonsen, our seven little children, and myself were seated at the table. We repeated the Lord's Prayer in unison, and when we came to the sentence, *Give us . . . our daily bread,* a feeling of fear flashed over my mind as to where our future dinners would come from; but I was enabled to look steadfastly to God. It was banished in an instant, and "a still small voice" said, *Fear thou not; for I am with thee: be not dismayed; for I am thy God: I will strengthen thee; yea, I will help thee; yea, I will uphold thee with the right hand of my righteousness* (Isaiah 41:10). At once I became conscious of a great sense of peace, joy, and assurance of God's constant loving care.

It was the day after New Year's when my good and noble wife and I set out to find a suitable house in a desirable location where we could start building our own little home nest. It was in the midst of a severe winter, with an abundance of snow, and was bitterly cold. We went forth, however, with hearts glad and grateful to our dear heavenly Father for His great goodness to us. We realized that God was lovingly opening the Red Sea, as it were, and leading us triumphantly through the dark and foreboding fears which surged about us.

Christian Science friends suggested that we take a house out in one of the suburbs, as the rent

would be less than right in the city where we had
decided to locate; but this did not appeal to me. I
stoutly affirmed to my well-meaning friends that
"When I gave up everything to go into Christian
Science, I did so because Christian Science stood
for something higher and better, in every sense of
the word, than what we had in the old thought.
I felt that it would mean progress all along the line
and not retrogression."

So we took a house on the same street where we
had been living, only nearer beautiful Prospect
Park. The experience we had in furnishing our new
home was most interesting. We found that as we
went boldly ahead and furnished it according to
what we felt was right for us to do, all went well;
but just the moment we halted and did not bring in
any more "vessels" (II Kings 4:6), the oil seemed to
cease flowing, until we broke up that sense of limitation and moved ahead as God opened the way
for us. But this was not always easy to do.

Of course, it was not long before the money
which Mrs. Simonsen had so lovingly placed at my
disposal as well as the money the kind friends in
my old church had given me, was gone; and we
stood with our seven dear little ones around us,
looking to us for food and raiment. To mortal sense
this did not look very bright, but we stood our

ground faithfully, and lovingly leaned on God. And these words kept ringing in my ears: *Trust in the Lord, and do good; so shalt thou dwell in the land, and verily thou shalt be fed* (Psalms, 37:3).

Some Christian Science friends also suggested that I take a position in an office until my practice should be sufficient to support us. I said: "No, I did not give up the ministry and the preaching of the Gospel of Christ, to go into business; I know God can and will care for us even better than in the old church." This, however, had to be demonstrated through divine Science. It did not come in a day, neither did it come before we were absolutely without a penny in the world. We stood without any material means whatsoever. Error tried to argue, of course, that we could not give ourselves and children even milk and gruel; for where would it come from? My indebtedness was piling up rapidly, but my credit, fortunately, was good. We found that if we even glanced at the material side of the question, darkness, fear, and despair stood like hungry beasts ready to devour us; but they did not, because we realized that—*He* [God] *is a shield unto them that put their trust in him* (Prov. 30: 5).

I recall one night, after the dear little ones were put to bed happy and without a care or worry to trouble their little breasts, that Mrs. Simonsen and

I sat down and talked over the situation fully. We realized that if we once began to curtail and economize in things we needed, that error, ere long, would manacle us with chains of limitation and despair. We therefore aroused ourselves through faithful mental work, realizing more clearly the all-ness of God; and that our supply was not in matter or human personality, but in our dear heavenly Father, who, we knew, was abundantly able to furnish a table in the wilderness, and who was the same yesterday, today, and forever. So we decided to give our children, as well as ourselves, not only as good things as we had before coming into Christian Science, but a little better. By thus facing error fearlessly, we became conscious of greater liberty and freedom from a sense of limitation which was constantly biting at our heels.

But the question of support was not all. I soon discovered that we were a bright and shining target for error in very many ways. Persecution broke forth upon us. It seemed for a time that impersonal evil (for evil is always impersonal, although seeming to have expression through persons, places or objects) was trying its best to discover some avenue through which it could attack not only myself, but members of my family as well. Evidently it did not relish the fact that I had given up preaching the old orthodox ideas, had accepted the teachings of, and had publicly taken my stand for Christian Science.

When it became known generally that I had taken this step from an honest conviction, and had thus broken the "solidarity of the body and the unity of the spirit," as Dr. Buckley expressed it, error became furious against me and my family. It struck right and left, even at our very lives.

One Sunday afternoon, a few weeks after we were settled in our own home, two members from my old church called and were met by our eldest daughter who expressed regret that her mother and father were not at home. They enquired where they were, and she explained that they had gone to New York with her brother to attend a Christian Science lecture at Carnegie Hall. They asked, "Your mother too?" My daughter replied, "Why, yes." They said nothing further about the purpose of their call to her, but they later told me they had been informed that Mrs. Simonsen had suddenly died, and they had called to express their sympathy.

A few months after this incident, I called on an old friend one morning, and as we stood talking in his office, one of his salesmen came in. When he saw me, he exclaimed, "Good morning, Mr. Simonsen, I am so glad to see you. It was not more than half an hour ago that one of the members of your former church asked me if I had heard that Mr. Simonsen had died suddenly." Error continued to strike at us through some of our children, manifesting itself when one boy was brought home in an unconscious condition on two different occasions, and afterwards reported in the papers to have been drowned.

Through our understanding of Christian Science we were enabled to conquer these malicious attacks, however, and we rejoiced to know and realize that through it all God was ever by our side helping us over the many rough places and saying, *Be strong and of a good courage, fear not, nor be afraid of them: for the Lord thy God, he it is that doth go with thee; he will not fail thee, nor forsake thee* (Deuteronomy 31:6).

As soon as the reporters for the newspapers learned of the step I had taken, for I was, so far as I have been able to learn, the first of the twenty-eight thousand regularly ordained and active ministers of the Methodist Episcopal Church, North and South, to renounce Methodism for Christian Science, they became greatly interested and called on me. They not only wanted an interview, but a photograph of myself as well; and when I refused to give them a picture, one said, "Do let me have one, Mr. Simonsen; and if you positively refuse to give us one of yourself, will you not permit us to take a picture of your residence, or something in connection with you? You must realize that the public is deeply interested in a successful clergyman who has seen fit to give up his ministry in the Methodist Episcopal Church to go into Christian Science. It is an unheard of step." I thanked him and assured him that I was not after such publicity.

However, a short time after, the editor of the *Christian Science Sentinel,* Judge Hanna, quoted and favorably commented on some articles that had appeared in the *Nordiske Blade* (Brooklyn, N. Y.) and the New York *Sun* concerning the step I had taken, heading his article, "An Important Step," and stating, among other things, that he noted my conversion had not been a hasty one; neither was it taken before long investigation and actual proofs had left no other alternative than deep conviction of the truth embodied in Christian Science by the fruits experienced. The Judge most cordially extended the hand of fellowship, and wished me Godspeed in this my rebirth.

Following are the extracts referred to and republished in the *Christian Science Sentinel.*

"About two weeks ago, the Rev. S. E. Simonsen, pastor of the Methodist Episcopal Church on Carroll Street, handed in his resignation as its pastor, and withdrew from the Methodist Episcopal Church.

"This step was a complete surprise to all, and caused no little consternation and amazement among the people. In speaking of his resignation the pastor said: 'While I am profoundly grateful for all that has come to me through the Methodist Episcopal Church, I now feel that the time has come when, in simple justice to the church as well as myself, I must withdraw from the ministry and membership of the said church, and ask that the same take effect just as soon as you can conveniently release me, which I hope will be at the close of this quarter.'

"As an honest and conscientious truthseeker he chose to follow the light his investigation had brought him. We can perhaps imagine something of the tremendous struggle and agony of soul and mind that this pastor must have passed through before reaching so vital a conclusion as this.

"To take so important a step as this requires a developed and perfectly balanced character, and when it is carried out to its full extent, as in this case, it has a right to expect to be treated with the conscientiousness and respect, that men owe a dearly won conviction.

"It is something over fourteen years since Mr. Simonsen first came in contact with Christian Science. At that time he was preaching in La Crosse, Wisconsin, but was brought face to face with what appeared to be an abrupt termination of his ministry on account of sickness that several prominent physicians had given up all hope of curing.

"He was finally persuaded to try Christian Science, and was most wondrously healed in a few days, and received such health and strength that he has been able to work without interruption ever since and that in some very hard and difficult fields. But no real change in his theological views took place at this time; he remained satisfied with the teachings of his church and faithfully stood on this foundation all these years, putting all his power and energy into the very important work entrusted to him. But during this year, circumstances kindled anew the spark that had unconsciously laid smouldering in his heart. Circumstances were such that he had to seek help for one of his children, and as a last resort he went to Christian Science, and at the same time commenced anew to study their doctrines, life and practice. He soon became convinced that he had found the Truth, and the sequel of it all was, that he withdrew from the Methodist Episcopal Church.

"His resignation will be accepted as soon as the Bishop can find a suitable man to take his place.

"Mr. Simonsen has taken an active part in the work of his church for more than eighteen years. For more than nine years he has been laboring here in Brooklyn, where he has been respected and honored as an earnest and faithful minister and a gifted speaker. In return he only holds the best thoughts and kindly feelings for all, both high and low, in the church where he has labored for so many years."—*Nordiske Blade, December 14, 1900.*

"Next Sunday the Rev. Simonsen will preach his farewell sermon in the Methodist Episcopal Church in Carroll Street. He will be sure of a full house, for during all the years that Mr. Simonsen has labored here he has put his whole soul into the work and gained a large following. If there should be a few that are dissatisfied, we feel assured that all will have to unite in saying the pastor has walked openly and frankly and taken the Truth for his guide.

"As he withdraws from the church that he has served for such a long time, we feel assured that all will wish him a good and successful future."—*Nordiske Blade, December 28, 1900.*

"Last Sunday evening the Rev. Severin E. Simonsen preached his farewell sermon and withdrew from the Methodist Episcopal Church where he has been preaching so many years.

"The church was packed to its utmost capacity, as we might have expected, because here was a unique and unparalleled case in the history of the community. A case that was to receive its explanation and culmination, as well as unfolding a drama of a soul struggling for more light, laying itself open to public criticism, here was a problem to be solved that no doubt looked difficult and incomprehensible to many minds. After Mr. Simonsen had given a short sketch of his labors here, and the condition of the church, he told about his withdrawal from the Methodist Church and his determination to join the ranks of the Christian Scientists.

"Our readers are fully conversant with the important step that Mr. Simonsen has just taken, and we think that his personal explanation last Sunday evening must have convinced every one present that his change must have been the fruit of an honest and candid searching for the Truth, and that it became absolutely necessary for him to make this complete change, if he would be true to his conscientious conviction. We feel confident that those who may have come with doubt in their minds as to his honesty of purpose went away convinced of his sincerity, and also that this difficult problem was cleared up in the minds of all, and that his many friends received another proof of Mr. Simonsen's honesty and fidelity to the Truth." *Nordiske Blade, January 4, 1901.*

The following is republished from the New York *Sun.*

"The Rev. Severin E. Simonsen, for nearly twenty years a minister of the Methodist Church, has withdrawn from the denomination and resigned the pastorate of the Norwegian Methodist Church in Carroll Street, Brooklyn, to become a Christian Scientist. The Rev. Simonsen has had charge of the Carroll Street Church for the past ten years and was well known in religious circles. In his letter of resignation to the Rev. Dr. J. S. Chadwick, Presiding Elder of his district, he said:

" 'I have been forced by circumstances to make an honest and impartial investigation into the teachings and practice of Christian Science, and I have found them to be in accordance with the teachings of Christ, and capable of such clear demonstration that to my mind no honest and impartial mind can conscientiously ignore or disregard them when once understood. I therefore must accept them, or do violence to my honest and highest conviction that God has given me.' He said, 'I freely choose to follow this God-given light, for it was through

Christian Science that I was given back my health, when a number of eminent physicians had given me up. And this was not all. There came to me a spiritual insight into the Word and power of God, the like of which I have never known until I came in touch with the Truth as taught by these people.'

"The sickness to which Rev. Mr. Simonsen refers, occurred, he said, about fourteen years ago when he was a minister in Wisconsin. He was at the point of death, he says, when he accepted the services of a Christian Science healer and quickly recovered. Four years later he was cured in a similar manner, he says, of an attack of scarlet fever."

In the beginning, I of course did not have any patients, and I therefore had a splendid opportunity to devote my time to the study of the Bible and *Science and Health.*

Gradually patients began to come to me for treatment, but they were nearly all of the poorer class, who thought they were not able to pay for their treatments. Friends lovingly sent me patients, but they, too, were mostly of the same kind. The people who could pay were usually sent to those who had an established practice; but I was grateful for any one who came seeking the Truth honestly; I say honestly because I have learned through my long experience, that it is of vital importance for a patient desiring healing in Christian Science to seek it righteously. I will relate the following instance to show this is true.

A lady doctor, who was somewhat interested in Christian Science, came to me one day, and told me about a very poor and destitute man with quite a large family. She said it was a bad case of cancer. He had been in a hospital twice, and had undergone two operations. The third time he went there, they again cut him open; but when they found him in such a bad condition that nothing could be done for him, they sewed him up and sent him home to die. This lady doctor told him about Christian Science, and he bespoke a desire to try it. She therefore asked me if I would take the case, to which I gladly consented. I went there on a Saturday afternoon and treated him. He was in bed, and had been suffering much pain. On the following Tuesday he was up and around in the house. The last of the week he was out on the street, much to the amazement of his neighbors, who expected to see him carried out to Greenwood Cemetery any day. In two weeks he was so well and strong that he went down to see his former employer about getting back to work again. He also called on our mutual friend, the doctor. Then he came to see me and told me what he had been doing. I informed him I did not want him to be calling on any doctor as long as he was under my care. He said, "But she is so interested in my case." I replied, "I know that, but do not do it again."

I found out later that the good doctor had called up some of her medical friends immediately, and told them about this cancer case which was now under Christian Science treatment. They agreed that it would not last and that he would have a relapse. The next day—Sunday—it came. Finding himself in great pain he sent out and procured a drug which he had been in the habit of taking to quiet his pain. After he had taken the drug he sent for me, but told me nothing about his use of it. He grew steadily worse, but still he said nothing.

Finally a good Christian Science lady who had volunteered to come in and nurse him, and care for the little children while his wife went out to work, found a small phial of this drug in his bed. Even then he was not honest enough to tell her the truth, but said he kept it in his bed so the children could not get hold of it. When I came and was told about it, he stoutly denied taking any of the drug. I did not feel that he was telling me the truth, and I told him so, further stating I would have to give up his case. Then he owned up and begged me to stay with him. He gave me the phial and made me believe he would not use it again. I then went on with his case and he improved, until suddenly he had another relapse. Then I gave up the case; for I knew he was not honest with God and myself.

The next day the doctor came and begged me to go out and help him again. He had confessed to her all about his seeming dishonesty. I responded once more. We had the same experience for the third time. He said, "The pain, Mr. Simonsen, comes when you are not here and I have to take it." I felt sorry for the dear man. Finally I told him I would stay right there with him day and night for a time and break up this condition if he would do his part and be honest with me, and not take anything. He refused. Later he told his wife and the doctor that he did not think God would require so much of him as Mr. Simonsen did. Then, of course, I was obliged to give up the case. It was only a few days, however, before he found that the drug did not help him at all, and the man passed out in great agony. *And Asa . . . was diseased . . . until his disease was exceeding great: yet in his disease he sought not the Lord, but to the physicians. And Asa . . . died* (II Chronicles Chap. 16).

The healing power of Truth is available when the power and presence of God is held to, as is beautifully evidenced by the following case brought to me—that of a young lady—who had a bone cancer, but was honest, and who clung steadfastly to

God through all she had to endure before she received her healing. She had been the recipient of two beautiful healings before this one, namely, tuberculosis and ptomaine poisoning. It did not come, however, before she was willing to submit to remaining in her room, and to forego the pleasure of seeing more than two or three friends now and then. The reason for this seclusion was that her seeming condition was so repulsive, and made itself so real to the material senses of people, that the fewer who saw her, the better. It was hard, but she took up the cross bravely, and we won out again, although friends advised me to give up the case, saying it could not be met, and that I would only get myself into trouble. I replied, "I will never forsake a patient as long as he needs me and wants me to help him, come what may." Nothing came but good, and she was beautifully healed.

CHAPTER VI

THE ECCLESIASTICAL STORM

UST as I was in the midst of demonstrating supply, and further proving that the teachings I had accepted were the Truth, and nothing but the Truth, I also had to meet the third question I had in mind when I entered the class in Christian Science, namely, "Could Christian Science enable me to meet the ridicule and persecution I would encounter by taking this radical stand for Christian Science?" As I sat in that class and saw and realized how beautifully my first two questions had been answered and settled beyond the shadow of a doubt, I thought to myself that the third question would not trouble me in the least, so I let it rest there.

I soon found, however, that this question was more serious than I had contemplated, and that it was not to be lightly brushed aside. This, too, I found had to be met and mastered scientifically.

My old Conference—the New York East—met in Brooklyn, New York, in April, the following Spring;

and when my resignation came up before that body for action, as is the custom when a Methodist minister withdraws to join another denomination, it was greeted with a storm of ridicule and persecution, which in turn spread throughout the Methodist Church, and also to other denominations as well.

The prolonged discussions which followed the reading of my resignation, caused many remarks—kind and otherwise—to be made concerning Christian Science, and its Discoverer and Founder, and one who had had the courage of his God-given conviction to take his stand for what he saw and realized was the Truth.

I am happy to say, however, that my dear heavenly Father enabled me to see that all these attacks were impersonal—error striking at Truth. By realizing their unreality, and making them stepping-stones to something higher and better, I learned that if persecution is met in the right way, it elevates and purifies. Note the exemplification in the lives of Daniel, Paul, and others of Biblical history. Christ said, *Blessed are ye, when men shall revile you, and persecute you, and shall say all manner of evil against you falsely, for my sake. Rejoice, and be exceeding glad: for great is your reward in heaven: for so persecuted they the prophets which were before you* (Matthew 5:11, 12).

In narrating some of the many things that were said and done in connection with my resignation, I wish to emphasize the fact that I do it not only without any resentment whatsoever, and with only love in my heart for one and all, but also without any desire to criticize, judge, condemn or injure any one. I simply relate it because it is a component part of my experience from the Methodist Pulpit into Christian Science, and because it is so intimately connected with the step I took, that it cannot be left out consistently. I feel it is only just to the reader of this message of love to insert a few of the events. It only shows how good men may be misled at times in their zeal for what they think is right and their duty to say and do,—just as Saul of Tarsus did before he gained a better and higher understanding of God and His Christ. But when this light and understanding dawned upon Saul, and he realized what he was really doing, he changed his course at once; so will we all do if we are as conscientious as he was.

The great dailies of New York and in other parts of the country reported these attacks more or less in full and always with glaring headlines. As I now reread these journalistic accounts, they appear amusing and it is almost unbelievable that such incidents could have occurred only a quarter of a century ago. But it is another example of how religious history repeats itself; for it was only a few decades prior to this event that the leaders of the Church of England persecuted John Wesley, the Founder of Methodism, and his followers, because they did not share his enlightened views and interpretations of the Scriptures, in like manner as did the orthodox churches with Mrs. Eddy, when she first proclaimed her discovery of Christian Science.

The following may well serve as a specimen of both headlines and contents of these reports:

"The Rev. Simonsen's resignation read in the New York East Conference contained a presentment for Christian Science and created a furor."

CHRISTIAN SCIENCE STIRS METHODIST EPISCOPAL CONFERENCE SESSION

Adherents of That Faith Arraigned During Debate Over Mr. Simonsen's Withdrawal

REFUSED HIS CREDENTIALS

Parchment Will Be Placed in the Archives of the Conference, etc.

One of the New York great dailies stated:

"The storm broke when the Presiding Elder of the Brooklyn, South District, the Rev. Dr. James S. Chadwick, read his report and came to that part of it where he related the circumstances regarding the withdrawal from the Methodist ministry of the Rev. Severin E. Simonsen, formerly pastor of the Norwegian Church, Brooklyn, in favor of Christian Science. The matter came up in Dr. Chadwick's report, as it was necessary for him to read the letter of withdrawal of Mr. Simonsen and the reasons given therefor.

"The letter of the Rev. Mr. Simonsen is as follows:

" 'Brooklyn, New York,
" 'November 29, 1900.

" 'Rev. James S. Chadwick,
" 'Presiding Elder of Brooklyn, South District,
" 'New York East Conference.

" 'DEAR BROTHER:

" 'While I am profoundly grateful for all that has come to me through the Methodist Episcopal Church, I now feel that the time has come when in simple justice to myself, I must withdraw from the membership and ministry of said church, and ask that the same take effect just as soon as you can conveniently release me, which I hope will be at the end of this quarter.

" 'The reason for this seeming radical step is this: I have been forced by circumstances to make an honest and impartial investigation into the teachings and practice of Christian Science, and I have found them to be in accordance with the teachings of Christ, and capable of such clear demonstration that, to my mind, no honest and impartial mind can conscientiously ignore or disregard them when once understood. I therefore must accept them or do violence to the highest and best conviction that God has given me, and I freely choose to follow this God-given light, for it was through Christian Science that I was given back my health when a number of eminent physicians had given me up. But this was not all. There came to me such a spiritual insight into the Word, and such a power from God, the like of which I had never known until I came in touch with the Truth as taught by these people.

" 'I wish to thank the New York East Conference for the love and good-will that I have enjoyed during the years that I have had the honor to be a member of this esteemed body.

" 'I will surrender my credentials as soon as I am released from further service. I respectfully ask that the Conference will kindly return the same to me in accordance with paragraph 161 of the Discipline.

" 'Yours as ever, for the cause of Christ,

" 'SEVERIN E. SIMONSEN.' "

The paragraph referred to in the letter and on which the discussion arose is as follows:

"When a minister in good standing withdraws to join the ministry of another church his credentials should be surrendered to the Conference, and, if he shall desire, may be returned to him."

Presiding Elder Chadwick said that he thought the parchments should be returned. The brother had done good work in the church for many years, and while it was true that he did not go to a recognized orthodox church, it was an organization, and he could not see how the returning of his credentials would in any way reflect on the Conference. "'Mr. Simonsen," said Dr. Chadwick, "wants to retain them only as souvenirs of his past life in the church. We want to recognize in some way a request that comes from a minister who has so long been a faithful servant of God and of the Methodist Episcopal Church."

The Bishop was asked his opinion concerning the return of the credentials, to which he replied, he was not there to define the rule, but to enforce it. By the reading of the paragraph, he said he did not see that the credentials could be returned.

Dr. Pullman thought the whole matter was in the hands of the Bishop, and he should decide whether the Conference could pass final judgment on the standing of Christian Scientists.

The Rev. Herbert Welch quoted the passage, *For where two or three are gathered together in my name, there am I in the midst of them,* as meaning a New Testament Church, and though he was not in sympathy with Christian Science teachings, he knew the Scientists believed in Jesus Christ.

In reply to a request for Bishop Fitzgerald to define a Christian Church he said: "The Church is the whole body of God's true people in every period of time. If these Scientists are God's true people then they are a part of the church."

"For the Lord's sake and our manliness," said one minister, "let's give him back his parchments."

Drs. Pullman and Downie and others strenuously opposed any sort of recognition, direct or indirect.

Dr. Adams took a broader view, and said, "Let's give the poor boy back his parchments. He wants a souvenir of what he has been." And Dr. Adams further said, "Suppose after fifty-three years of straight ahead work in the ministry I wanted to go

into the Christian Science Church. If I asked for
my papers would this Conference stand up and say,
'Old Ben Adams shall not have his parchments'?"
(Cries of "Yes, yes.")

Professor Rice, of Wesleyan University, main-
tained that the Conference, as a representative
body of the Methodist Episcopal Church, could not
afford in any way or manner to recognize the Christian Scientists, and he earnestly hoped it would
not be done.

Dr. Downie made a motion to the effect that
"while we repudiate his interpretation of Christian
Science, we accept his withdrawal."

An amendment by Dr. Williams, providing that
the parchments be not returned to Mr. Simonsen,
but filed in the archives of the Conference, was accepted by Dr. Downie. The motion was then passed
with about six opposing. At the next morning session Drs. Rice, Welch, now a bishop, and Upham
brought in the following resolution:

"Whereas, Brother Severin E. Simonsen has
withdrawn from the ministry and membership of
the Methodist Episcopal Church, and

"Whereas, under the law of the church we are
unable to surrender his parchments to him,

"Resolved, that we hereby record our appreciation of his personal worth and years of faithful

service, and regret that he feels compelled to leave us." The resolution was passed unanimously.

This action on the part of the Conference, to my mind, really reflected the true and Christian spirit of the assembly as a whole; while the following incident may serve to show how one influential member of a group of men, if he is an able debater, eloquent and persuasive speaker, can sometimes sway the whole body to his line of reasoning.

A little later the same day, this action of the Conference was strenuously opposed by Dr. James M. Buckley, editor of the New York *Christian Advocate,* who had been absent from the Conference up to this moment, and who upon his arrival at the meeting plainly stated he had traveled all night to be able to appear and defeat a resolution of this kind. He requested that the vote of appreciation and regret be rescinded.

Dr. Downie expressed the opinion that it would be wise to avoid further discussion of Christian Science, for he had, no doubt, awakened to the fact that such a course would not redound to the good of the cause of Christ.

Dr. Buckley was allowed to go on, however, and said, "I do not believe that any one who has left us to go over to Christian Science should receive any resolution of regret from us. Up to the time that our brother was infected with the bacilli of Christian Science he was a manly preacher of the Word of God, genial and a serious-minded brother. I respected him highly and rejoiced to call him friend. But when a man leaves us to join an organization which is absolutely opposed to the doctrines of the Church and Christianity, I believe that we should be glad that he has left the ministry rather than remain in it with these doctrines. Mr. Simonsen, I understand, harboured the teachings of Christian Science in his mind and was thinking about them for four years before he became an outspoken member of the organization. He has been treated with the utmost consideration, has been accorded the Elder's indulgence in that he was allowed to remain pastor of his church, after the Presiding Elder knew that his views were out of accord with that church."

The Rev. Dr. Chadwick, Presiding Elder of the district in which Mr. Simonsen's charge was located, rose to his feet at this point and said that the matter was one which called for an explanation. "That's right," replied Dr. Buckley good humoredly, "what I say to your face many others have said behind your back."

Dr. Chadwick explained that when he had first learned of Mr. Simonsen's change of faith, he had been deeply concerned for more reasons than one. Mr. Simonsen was a pastor of a Norwegian congregation and his parishioners were deeply attached to him. "His change of mind was entirely unexpected by me, and I desired a further interview with him. When I discovered that his mind was made up, I called in the nearest bishop and advised with him. Mr. Simonsen had the confidence of all of us, and I did not have another man who could serve in his place. Mr. Simonsen was allowed to hold over for about four weeks, or until another preacher could be secured."

The Presiding Elder explained with some emotion that he had been "guided in his actions solely with an eye to the good of the church." He was heartily applauded.

Dr. Buckley continued his former remarks and said: "I am opposed to granting this expression of approval from ourselves, because the teachings of the sect which he has embraced deny and ridicule every doctrine which we hold sacred, including even that of purity." He further said: "This man must have undergone a mysterious mental and moral change. If you say he has not, you undermine the whole foundation on which we stand. I say that the man who can pass into this state of mind, remaining with us, would be a curse to the denomination; and the man who regrets that he leaves us is preparing for the same position. I do not mean that he is preparing to become a Christian Scientist, but to exert an influence unfavorable in every way to the solidarity of the body and the unity of the spirit. To give this man a recommendation would be to act as a doting father does who leaves his wayward son all he possesses. Atheists cannot do as much harm, in my opinion, as can Christian Scientists. They are a mischievous abomination. We should count ourselves well rid of this man."

According to the rules of the Conference the Doctor had only ten minutes in which to address the body. But the doctor was the idol of the Conference and was granted thirty minutes in which to speak. He was the recognized leader not only of this Annual Conference, but of the General Conference of the Methodist Episcopal Church as well. He was a brilliant man, a most fluent, interesting, and entertaining speaker. He invariably held his audience spellbound, no matter what his subject might chance to be. The Doctor was a unique and powerful figure in the whole church.

Dr. Downie was a close second to this gifted and popular orator. I loved them both, as I did all of these grand men who labored faithfully and no doubt conscientiously for their Master.

Dr. Buckley finally persuaded the Conference to rescind the motion, but the vote was not unanimous.

At a Methodist ministers' meeting in New York City a few days after the close of the Conference, the preachers listened to a paper on Christian Science by Dr. E. P. Odell, who delivered the formal address. At the close of it, Dr. J. W. Johnson, member of the New York East Conference, said something which was rather interesting, as did also Dr. Lawrence of the same Conference. The remarks of both these men show that the leaven of a more liberal and brotherly feeling was evidently at work in their hearts, and we give thanks to our dear heavenly Father for the manifestation of more of the true Christ, Spirit.

According to one of the New York papers, Dr. Johnson said: "I have known of several most earnest and devout Methodists who have gone over to the Christian Scientists and it has amazed me to see how, in the light of their faith and the conduct of their lives, they have testified to the good they have received. I confess I am perplexed. There is something in it, or it would not occupy the place in the community it does today."

This same paper quoted Dr. W. H. Lawrence as saying: "The Methodists are likely to suffer more than any other denomination from Christian Science because they emphasize the spiritual exaltation that the Methodists claim to enjoy."

Just after this, some of the good churchmen tried to work up a concerted action against Christian Science in Brooklyn, New York. This failed, however, because the more liberal and broad-minded among them pointed out to their brethren that this would only be a benefit to the Christian Science Church, as it no doubt would cause many of their members to look into the subject. They were right, for many good pillars in the orthodox churches received their first incentive to investigate the teachings of Christian Science while listening to a criticism of Christian Science by their pastors. I have met a number of such cases in my experience.

I recall a gentleman from Maryland, who was a prominent official in the Methodist Church, and who first had his curiosity aroused about Christian Science from hearing a vigorous sermon against it by his pastor. He decided at once to investigate, and found it so to his liking that he resigned from the Methodist Church, went into Christian Science, and became a successful practitioner.

Much good came to Christian Science, and people generally, through these many interesting discussions concerning Christian Science, its Leader, and of those who followed her God-inspired teachings, because of the Christlike manner in which the Christian Scientists always met these attacks. The public press also woke up to see that it was wrong to publish articles against a body of Christian people who humbly and faithfully preached the Gospel of Christ, and healed the sick in Jesus' way. There was a pleasing and most decided reaction in favor of tolerance and fair play from this on.

One of the editors of a leading New York paper interviewed me at the time of Dr. Buckley's attack, and asked me why we did not "bring him to terms." I told him that was not the way we treated an opponent in Christian Science. The Doctor and all others who had said anything against Christian Science and its teachings would have to answer to their heavenly Father. We have nothing but love for all men, and we try to practice the Sermon on the Mount, which is the sum and substance of Christian Science. Christ said, *But I say unto you, Love your enemies, bless them that curse you, do good to them that hate you, and pray for them which despitefully use you, and persecute you"* (Matthew 5:44).

It was rather amusing though, to see how some people who had been my friends and co-workers for years, did not seem at first to even know me after I had left the Methodist ministry; but this wore off after a time, and love prevailed. I also received a number of anonymous letters couched in most abusive terms, and some even threatened my life. But on the other hand there were many interesting and favorable comments in the public press commending the stand that I had taken.

The following article, quoted from a contributor to the New Haven *Leader*, will serve as a sample of the more liberal thought then making itself felt throughout the country on religious tolerance.

"In a late issue of your paper Dr. Buckley denounces Christian Science. It seems this denunciation was precipitated upon Christian Science through the resignation from the ministry of the Methodist Episcopal Church of the Rev. Severin E. Simonsen. It would appear to the reading public, by the remarks of Dr. Buckley, that this man has committed an unpardonable sin because he has repudiated Methodism and turned to Christian Science. Is it a crime for a man to acknowledge a change of mind on a matter of religion? I think not. He is rather to be commended for taking a bold stand in the face of all opposition, for his honest convictions, born as they are from experience.

"The Rev. Severin E. Simonsen gave very fair and candid reasons for taking the step he did. He said, 'I have been forced by circumstances to make an honest and impartial investigation into the teachings of Christian Science, and found them to be in accordance with the teachings of Christ, and capable of such clear demonstration that to my mind, no honest or impartial mind can conscientiously ignore or disregard them when once understood. It was through Christian Science that I was given back my health when a number of eminent physicians had given me up. But this was not all. There came to me such a spiritual insight into the Word, and such a power of God, the like of which I had never known until I came in touch with the Truth as taught by these people.'

"Is Dr. Buckley manifesting the spirit of our dear Master in his arraignment of this honest, conscientious man for turning from dogma and creed to serve the living and true God, according to his own conviction, from his former faith to the understanding that God *healeth all our diseases;* and *forgiveth all our iniquities?*

"This man has tested both systems. Is he not capable of deciding which produces the results he needs? It appears to me that the man who has studied both sides of the question from an unbiased standpoint is qualified to judge its merits.

"Dr. Buckley said, 'Up to the time Mr. Simon sen was infected with these bacilli of Christian Science he was a serious minded, genial brother. I respected him highly and rejoiced to call him my friend.'

"Unfortunately for Dr. Buckley's peace of mind, this infection has spread so rapidly within the past year, throughout the United States and Canada, that the New York Independent rates its increase nine hundred and twenty thousand. Our Methodist brethren have no occasion to feel disturbed over the matter, for if this work be of man, it will come to naught, but if it be of God, *the gates of hell shall not prevail against it*."

As a further indication of the more liberal attitude held by some of the clergymen of the day, I herewith quote extensively from a sermon by a Congregational minister, Rev. Dr. T. DeWitt Talmage Van Doran of Brooklyn, N. Y., which was published in one of the daily newspapers.

"The criticisms of New York clergymen of different denominational views published in today's *Journal*, concerning Christian Science as a religion, are not nearly as damaging to that cult as to the Christian Churches, if it be true that these criticisms represent the spirit of evangelical Christianity. I am not in any sense a follower of Mrs. Eddy; indeed there is much in her teachings that does not appeal to me as being true; yet, at the same time there is much that must command the respect and admiration of every candid and unprejudiced mind.

"These criticisms may be well meant. They doubtless express the honest convictions of the authors, who feel called upon, as a matter of conscience, to warn the masses against an, to them, insidious and deadly enemy to the highest interests of humanity.

"Nevertheless, they were unwise, as they must inevitably react upon the churches represented by these critics. *He that takes the sword shall perish with the sword. For with what judgment ye judge ye shall be judged; and with what measure ye mete it shall be measured to you again. Whatsoever a man sows that shall he also reap.* There is no escape from this law. *Be not deceived, God is not mocked.*

"These criticisms are untimely, since they disclose a temper inimical to the spirit and teachings of Jesus Christ, whose servants all ministers are supposed to be, and whose spirit they are supposed to imitate. They reveal sensitiveness, amounting to almost irritability, toward an institution which seems to them to threaten the 'tradition of the elders.'

"On the other hand, the spirit manifested by the Christian Science advocates is in strange and happy contrast to the spirit of these theological archers.

Being defamed, they still entreat their critics to deal kindly and candidly with them, since they desire naught but the furtherance of the Truth. The world at large will not be slow to discern the spirit of Christ in the attitude of this church.

"Why should clergymen think it is a wrong thing, and contrary to the preaching of Christ, that a church should believe in and practice bodily healing? Christ was the sickness bearer of his people. *Himself took our infirmities and bore our sicknesses. Thy sins be forgiven thee* and *be whole of thy plague.*

"The ministry of the apostles, under the leadership of the Spirit, is the exact model of the Master's. Nor did this commission end with the death of the Apostles, for Mark says, *These signs shall follow them that believe,* not the immediate Apostles of Christ only, but all believers, in every generation of the Church's history.

"If the practice of healing the sick is the basis of suspicion against the Christian Science Church, it can well afford to rest under the suspicion, since it has the sanction of Jesus Christ, and also that of the Christian Church of all ages, for there never has been a period in the history of the church when there was not found these signs and wonders in response to faith.

"It is admitted that Christian Scientists represent the wealth and intelligence of the communities wherein they flourish. This fact ought to have some weight in any just estimate of motive and character.

"If the Christian Science Church has been instrumental in healing one million cases of sickness, or one thousand, ought not this to be taken into consideration by those who profess to believe in the healing power of Christ, and in the great commission, *Go, preach the Gospel and heal the sick?*

"The only class of people for whom Christ had words of biting sarcasm and censure were the Pharisees, who could not see any good in anything outside of Judaism. Are we not in danger of falling into the spirit of the Pharisees when we grow intolerant of the methods and beliefs of those who conscientiously differ from us, and who are still putting forth noblest effort for the physical and moral elevation of humanity?

"I have not the pleasure of Mrs. Eddy's acquaintance, but from all the evidence at hand I am obliged to think of her as a woman of remarkable ability and spotless character. I am bound to concede and respect her virtues of character, her intellectual ability, her right to worship God according to the dictates of her conscience, and to build up a great church if she can, and evidently she can.

"I have met and known personally a number of Mrs. Eddy's followers, and in every way they compared favorably with the highest type of Christians found in my own church. How shall we judge the merits of a church if not by the type of Christians it turns out? *By their fruits ye shall know them.*

"When it is understood by the whole people that the objective point of the churches is character rather than wealth, the problem how to reach the 'better class' will be solved, for the world is not slow to distinguish between an orthodox Christian and an orthodox Pharisee. While it loves and honors the one, it has only abhorrence and detestation for the other.

"If the Christian Science Church, or any other church, no matter what its name, generates the most of the spirit of Christ in feeling and conduct, that church will triumph in the end. God forbid that it should be truthfully said of the Christianity of the twentieth century, that it is just as conceited and arrogant in its day as were the Pharisees in their day. They despised the Gentiles. Shall we despise men because they are not of our sect?

"*In Jesus Christ neither circumcision availeth anything nor uncircumcision, but faith, that works by love.* If this young and thriving organization, known to the Orthodox Christianity by an unfamiliar, and, to it, harsh sounding name, bears the fruits of the spirit, *Love, joy, peace, long-suffering, gentleness, goodness, faith, meekness, temperance,* it comes within the intention and spirit of Jesus Christ and is entitled to recognition as a Church of Christ.

"And whether it does or does not has nothing to do with the evident duty of Christian Churches centuries old. It is our duty to set an example of toleration and of goodness, of kindness, of forbearance, of love, to all the world. It is our duty to manifest the spirit of Jesus Christ. *Peace on earth, good will toward men: until we all come in the unity of the faith, and the knowledge of the Son of God, unto a perfect man, unto the measure of the stature of the fullness of Christ."*

Today I find the thought among a number of the old members of the New York East Conference, and other like associations, has changed very greatly toward Christian Science and its adherents.

Some of the members of the different Conferences have called on me and discussed the subject in a most friendly way. Only a few days past, one of the foremost members of my old Conference, now the pastor of an English-speaking Methodist Church in one of the capitals of Europe, and also Vice-President of their college in the same city, remarked that he saw no reason for criticizing any one for accepting Christian Science if it met the need of the heart and if it brought God and His Christ into their lives more clearly. Discussing our literature, he volunteered the statement he considered the *Christian Science Monitor* the best English daily published in the world; and that he would be glad to receive it and place it in the library of their Methodist College, the same as some other Methodist institutions, to my knowledge, have done.

Another late instance was a happy reunion with one of the oldest and most prominent members of the New York East Conference, who stated with much emphasis that he was glad he had lived to an age wherein he had come to see and realize that discussions such as took place in the old Conference, at the time of my resignation, had no place among the followers of Christ.

I cannot be too deeply grateful to God that the seeming misunderstanding of a quarter of a century ago, as to what Christian Science really is, and its aim and purpose, has been largely eliminated from a majority of the orthodox Christian denominations and institutions of learning. That they have come to see Christian Science more in its true light, and that they realize Christian Scientists, too, are striving for the redemption of mankind, has not only wrought a closer association and a deeper interest in the tenets of Christian Science, but is evidenced as well by the deep and widespread regard shown for the Christian Science literature and the privileges granted students forming Christian Science Societies within their institutions of learning.

I herewith quote in full the contents of a letter from one informant that covers much the same information as comes to me from many sources, and illustrates much of what is occurring all over the country. Indeed the letter is doubly pleasurable to me, in that it reports my old Alma Mater, Garrett Biblical Institute, where I studied for the Methodist ministry, as appreciating to the fullest extent the periodicals of Christian Science and its great daily newspaper.

The letter is as follows:

"Evanston, Illinois
"December 6, 1926.

"Dear Mr. Simonsen:

"The privilege of answering your letter of November 21st gives me a deep sense of pleasure, because I know that what I have to tell you will make you happy.

"Gift subscriptions to the *Monitor, Sentinel* and *Journal,* are being received at the Garrett Biblical Institute with more than ordinary interest. They are saving and filing the periodicals, and in other ways have expressed their interest and appreciation of the Christian Science literature.

"Gift subscriptions to the *Monitor* are being sent to the schools of Commerce and Economics; also to Lunt Library, as well as to all fraternity houses.

"You may also be interested to know that a special department of this committee is devoted to the mailing of literature to Northwestern University students known to be Christian Scientists. Letters expressing our willingness and readiness to send free literature to students who indicate their desire to receive it were sent to all.

"If you do not already know, you will be glad to learn that a Christian Science Society was formed at Northwestern University about a year ago.

"With kind regards,

> "Yours most sincerely,
>> "(Mrs.) A. D. F.,
>>> "Chairman
>> "Literature Distribution Committee."

I had preached my final sermon on the last Sunday night of the old century and stepped out of the Methodist Episcopal Church and Ministry. Mrs. Simonsen had also taken her stand and withdrawn from the membership of the church.

The next Sunday morning we took our little family to First Church of Christ, Scientist, in Brooklyn, New York, where we worshipped God in the light of our new-found faith and higher understanding of divine worship, and our children attended the Sunday School until we moved to New Haven, Connecticut, in the early part of 1902. Here we continued to reside and labor for our Master until 1920 when divine Love opened the way for us to come to sunny California, and live in the beautiful city of Los Angeles, with more than twenty large and beautiful Christian Science Churches.

How radically changed everything seemed to me. I was no longer in the pulpit preaching to others, but was privileged to sit with my dear family in the audience and listen to an impersonal sermon. The subjects were all chosen by Mrs. Eddy, the Discoverer and Founder of Christian Science, after she had ordained the Bible and *Science and Health with Key to the Scriptures* as the Pastor of her church.

We found the services most interesting, helpful, and inspiring.

CHAPTER VII

THE METAPHYSICAL COLLEGE AND THE
COMMUNION SEASON

FTER THE STORM the calm, beautiful sunshine, invigorating and refreshing air. In May, 1901, Mrs. Eddy lovingly invited me, through the Board of Directors of The Mother Church, to attend the normal class of the Metaphysical College in June. Mrs. Eddy did not send me a card of free tuition to this class, as I have been told she had often done with clergymen in the past. This, however, did not trouble me in the least. In fact, I considered it a compliment that Mrs. Eddy had the confidence in my ability to make the demonstration without her financial assistance.

Some time later I learned that my primary teacher, who was with Mrs. Eddy a great deal, had told Mrs. Eddy about my family and financial condition, and suggested to her that it would be lovely, if she thought best, to give me a free tuition card.

Mrs. Eddy replied, "Please keep your hands off of Mr. Simonsen and let me handle his case."

As I made ready to go to Boston to study in the Metaphysical College, I found that God had provided beautifully for my family's need during my absence in that city; also the best new outfit of clothing for myself that I had ever enjoyed, money for my railroad fare, and room and board while there. But error kept hounding me about the one hundred dollars for my tuition. Where was it coming from? I rested easy, for I knew I was leaning on God to provide for the need.

When I came home from my office an evening or two before I was to start for Boston, my dear wife handed me a letter addressed in a strange handwriting. I opened it and found enclosed a check for one hundred dollars, the amount needed for my tuition. The letter and check were from a member of First Church of Christ, Scientist, in Brooklyn, New York, saying among other things, that she was deeply interested in the stand I had taken for Christian Science, and as I was going to Boston to study she thought perhaps a little extra money would not be amiss, and would I accept it in the same spirit in which it was sent. With my heart overflowing with gratitude to God, Christian Science, and this good lady, I tucked the check in my inside pocket, and kept it intact, until I handed it to the Treasurer of the Board of Education.

The fact that I had to pay my own tuition the same as any other student, was a great blessing to me, greater than might appear on the surface. As a clergyman I had been the recipient of many special favors, because I was a minister of the Gospel, in the form of donations, half-fare rates on the railroads, special discounts, etc. This sort of thing had had the tendency to cultivate in the minds of the clergy the idea that they were a special class, entitled to special favors and privileges along every line. It was not elevating in the least, but this custom had evolved from the early days when clergymen were much more underpaid than they are now. In Christian Science this had all changed. Now I, too, could play the part of a real man, and pay my own way in full as did other men. It was a splendid thing for me, and I was more deeply grateful to God and Mrs. Eddy than words can express when I walked up the aisle of the Mother Church and paid my tuition in full.

In Boston I found beautiful quarters with a private family on Columbus Avenue, not far from where our Leader lived at one time.

The class was an unusually large one—eighty-one members—and representative in character, embracing, as it did, students from various parts of the globe. Twenty-one states of the Union, also China, England, Scotland, France, and Canada, were represented.

Our teacher, Mr. Edward A. Kimball, C. S. D., was to my mind the most able exponent of Christian Science that I have had the pleasure of listening to, except, of course, Mrs. Eddy. I have sat for months in class rooms listening to learned professors and able teachers, but I never supposed it to be possible for any human being to teach and unfold to his students, in the short space of two weeks, all that Mr. Kimball imparted to us about God, man, heaven, hell, the universe, angels, sin, sickness and death, Spirit and matter, the unfoldment of the Principle of Christian Science and how to apply it successfully to all human needs. His teachings were deep and comprehensive. To me he left nothing to be desired. His style was simple, clear, logical, convincing, and illuminating.

He was thoroughly imbued with the great Truth he unfolded. He seemed to sense the need of each student. With it all he was so humble and unassuming. Loyal to our Leader, he unfolded to us her God-given place in the scheme of the salvation of mankind.

At last I had found a teacher who was able to answer without begging from or evading any of the many important questions which he was called upon to answer. No wonder Mrs. Eddy loved him and deeply appreciated his understanding and correct teaching, his wise counselling, and the inspiration he instilled in all who came in contact with him, whether in class assemblies, or listening to his masterly lectures on Christian Science throughout the world.

I shall never cease to be grateful to God and our Leader for making it possible for me to attend this notable class and above all, for the higher understanding of the Truth that came to me during the sessions of the class, and has continued to unfold to me as I have progressed in the study of Christian Science. It has ever enabled me to help the many seekers after Truth who have come to me from time to time.

Before adjourning, the class sent a message of love and gratitude to Mrs. Eddy for the great privilege of attending this remarkable class. We also expressed to our teacher, Mr. Kimball, our deep appreciation of all he had done for us through his wonderful exposition of Christian Science.

The Communion and Annual Meeting of the Mother Church took place during the session of the class. This was my first experience in participating in a communion service in the Christian Science denomination. It was most interesting and helpful to me. It was so different from anything I had ever witnessed in the orthodox denominations. Its simplicity was beautiful and impressive. The love, peace, and joy that this vast throng of earnest Christian people reflected, impressed me deeply. You could not but feel and realize the unanimity of thought and action.

The closing of the class brought to each and every one of us the feeling that our spiritual hunger had been satisfied, and that the Truth had been revealed to us according to our ability to receive it.

Returning home from such a Pentecostal feast as we enjoyed during this class and communion season, one naturally took up his work with new vigor and higher inspiration than ever before. The healing of the sick and the sinful was accomplished more readily, for, of course, as one advances in the understanding of the allness of Good, he naturally realizes more clearly the nothingness of evil. Consequently my healing work unfolded more rapidly. The sense of limitation gave way somewhat; but the decisive test was yet to come.

CHAPTER VIII

MY VISIT TO MRS. EDDY

N SEPTEMBER, 1902, Mrs. Eddy was invited to visit the Concord Fair on a certain afternoon. She in turn invited the
First Members of her church and some
of the students to attend also. Mrs. Simonsen and
I were among the invited guests, and I am deeply
grateful to God that we were granted this wonderful privilege, for the visit was a great epoch in
our lives.

We arrived in Concord late Tuesday afternoon.
In the evening our primary teacher, who often
spent much time in the home of Mrs. Eddy, Mrs.
Simonsen and I strolled out toward Pleasant View.

It was a beautiful moonlight night, giving radiant charm to the setting as we secured our first
glimpse of Mrs. Eddy's home. It was a modest, yet
beautiful and attractive residence, with spacious
grounds, located on an eminent site overlooking
the valley, the city of Concord as well as the high-

lands of Bow in the distance. There was an unusually peaceful and harmonious atmosphere emanating from the domicile of the greatest advocate of true peace, love and harmony to this age, never to be forgotten.

The next day was a beautiful autumn day, with the golden foliage glittering in the warm sunshine. Concord was in her holiday attire because two honored guests were to appear at the Fair that afternoon, the Governor of the state, Honorable Chester B. Jordan, and our beloved Leader, Mrs. Eddy, who were present at the special invitation of the Officers of the Fair Association.

Mrs. Eddy's reception was dignified and most cordial, free from all spectacular or sensational features; but the spontaneous expression of the kindly feeling and the high esteem entertained for her by the officials of the State and the Fair, as well as the citizens of her native state, was visible on all sides.

We Christian Scientists deeply appreciated Governor Jordan's high commendation of our Leader's Christian character, as well as the cordiality with which Mr. Moses extended to her the freedom of the grounds.

That evening many of us attended the Wednesday evening meeting in the Concord Church. They worshipped in a small but attractive hall. Some years later Mrs. Eddy presented them with a beautiful church edifice which they now enjoy. This testimonial meeting was most interesting.

The next day Mrs. Simonsen and I were invited to visit Mrs. Eddy in her home. The house was well arranged for her convenience, modest but attractively furnished. She received us in her double parlor, and her reception was most cordial and loving. She appeared graceful, dignified, erect and queenly. Her costume was simple yet bespoke its quiet elegance. Leading the way with sprightly steps to a corner of the room, she graciously offered me a place on the divan beside her, seating Mrs. Simonsen comfortably in a chair in front and a little to her left.

I was most singularly impressed with the purity and beauty of her countenance, and her almost transparent face, so radiant with peace, joy, and love. But to me the most striking attraction was her wonderful eyes, the like of which I have never seen in all my experience of contact with people; they expressed volumes. It is beyond my power to describe how they responded to, and in various ways portrayed the sacred subject she would at the moment be discussing. You realized that she reflected the Christ mind so fully that she discerned without effort your mental state; but it did not disturb you. The sense that came to you was her desire not to injure, but to help and save—the same as our Master did when he discerned the thoughts of the people. Hence your heart filled with gratitude for such a helping hand.

There was almost a supernatural keenness to discern your innermost thoughts, but only for the purpose of helping, counseling and guiding you into a higher understanding of your heavenly Father. Yea, to bring out a more perfect confidence in God as your ever present help, and in your ability to do whatsoever God had for you to do.

Her talk with us and the instructions she gave were beautifully illuminating, deeply comprehensive, and wonderfully helpful—never to be forgotten. She took a deep interest in us, and showed us many gifts of love which some of her students had presented to her. One was a life-size painting of the Master as "The Good Shepherd." It was in the form of a banner. The Master stood with a shepherd's crook in his right hand, holding a little lamb up to his breast with his left arm. A little to the front and left stood the mother sheep, looking up into the shepherd's face with love and perfect confidence in the safety of her young. Back of the shepherd and to his right stood a flock of sheep, all looking up to the shepherd.

As we stood admiring the painting and its subject, Mrs. Eddy remarked: "See, how perfectly happy and contented they all seem? No crowding or pushing for place or position. They are all glad and willing to leave their future in the hands of their Shepherd."

Another picture which she said she prized very highly was the now famous English steel etching of "Daniel in the Lion's Den." As we stood before this most interesting picture she gave us a very entertaining and instructive explanation, not only of Daniel, but of the seven lions. Then she went on and told us that when error seemed to press her exceptionally hard, she would leave her work for a few minutes and come and stand before this picture, and study anew the calm and loving manner in which Daniel looked steadfastly to God and God only. He paid no heed to the lions or seeming danger, letting his dear heavenly Father care for the ferocious beasts and keep them at a safe distance. With new and fresh courage, she said, she would return to her work, with a heart full of joy and gratitude for His protecting care.

As we were standing looking out of her library window on the second floor, we had a remarkably fine view of Bow, New Hampshire. Pointing to her birthplace, Mrs. Eddy said smilingly, "Do you see

Bow over there? There is where they say, I was born."

She then turned and called our attention to a pretty little lake—a gift from her followers—on the estate, upon the surface of which a boat swung leisurely about; and with her wonderful graciousness she invited Mrs. Simonsen and me to come and enjoy a boat-ride whenever we desired.

The rich fragrance of her sweetness, love, and true Christian sympathy and interest in you, was a part of your legacy as you departed. It was, I am sure, of a like nature as the illumination and inspiration accorded the three disciples when, on the Mount, Moses and Elijah appeared and talked with the Saviour.

I cannot imagine how any impartial individual could sit at Mrs. Eddy's feet, and listen to her teaching, or even her talks on the subject of Christian Science, and not be thoroughly convinced that he was in the presence of the master-mind, ruled and governed entirely by the divine Mind.

Before it was my great privilege to be invited to visit her in her own home and listen to her, I used to wonder how it was that her faithful followers were so eager and conscientious in their endeavor to carry out her every wish and command. But after I met her personally, and came in contact with this great heart of love, it all became clear to me. I realized then that she manifested such Christ-love, such unselfed love for God and all mankind, and it was so apparent that she was divinely directed in all her efforts, that she required of her followers only that which was for the glory of God, their own unfoldment in Truth and Love, and the good of mankind.

It has been my privilege to meet and to listen to many of the foremost religious leaders of my time, both in this country and abroad; and I can truthfully say that in all my experience I have never met or listened to any one who, to my mind, reflected and manifested so fully the spirit and love of Christ as did Mrs. Eddy. I give thanks to God for all she has done, is doing, and will continue to do throughout the ages, both by her spoken and written word, for me and mine, for those whom I have been privileged to assist in the unfoldment of the Principle of Christian Science in their lives, and for all mankind.

I know of no words adequate to express fully my gratitude to God for this noble and wonderful woman, who was good enough, pure enough, unselfish enough, and intelligent enough to receive this revelation of divine Science, and to record it in such language as to make plain to the benighted understanding of mankind the way of God's full salvation through Christ.

This old and eternal Truth which has stood ready to heal man and save him from all forms of evil in every age, was especially made manifest by Jesus Christ. He put it into practice and taught his disciples how to heal the sick as well as the sinful, but it was lost sight of in the Third Century when Constantine popularized the Christian religion, and led it into worldliness and the loss of spiritual power.

It was left for an American woman of our time to rediscover the healing truth; and also to discover its laws and *modus operandi,* how to apply it to all human ills, be they physical, financial, social, political or spiritual, and to record the same in such plain and intelligent manner that *the wayfaring men though fools, shall not err therein* (Isaiah 35:8).

We are living in an age of great and important discoveries beneficial to mankind, which go to show something of man's God-given dominion. Why, then, should it be thought strange to find that the most important discoveries in the Nineteenth and Twentieth Centuries should be found on the higher or spiritual plane, especially when man realizes that his greatest need is also found on this plane?

At first both Mrs. Eddy and her writings were ignored by the public generally. Then as she demonstrated the Truth of her teachings by healing the sick and the sinful, she was ridiculed and scorned. But when her teachings began to spread and awaken a deep interest among the sick and the suffering, she was persecuted and maligned, not only by the public press and the different medical schools, but also by the Christian pulpit. But none of these things influenced her. She was so sure of her footing, and so deeply and thoroughly grounded in the position she had taken and in the Truth which she taught and demonstrated, that neither man nor devil could move her.

Furthermore, she was so abundantly able to deliver undeniable proof of the soundness of her teaching, and to demonstrate the unfailing Principle of divine Science, that she won her way to the front not only as an author but also as a true exponent of the teachings of Christ. She also proved her ability as Founder, Organizer, and Leader of the Christian Science movement, which she inaugurated in spite of all the prejudice and opposition she had to meet and overcome.

The Christ-like way in which she met, and taught her students to meet, the ridicule and persecution heaped upon them, will ever stand as a Christian example of how one should deal with his enemies. She always proceeded and advanced as she was able to establish her advancement, and protect it in God's own way, eliminating self and seeking only the glory of God, and the good of all mankind. Consequently she did not have to retrace her steps. She waited on God, as she has told us, and moved only as He moved. She was always on the alert to move just as fast as God opened the way for her and her followers. Like the Master, she had yet many things to tell her students, but she always waited for them to become ready for the advanced idea and forward step.

Her writings are clear, deep, comprehensive, and logical to all who get her viewpoint. I do not know of another author who can compare with Mrs. Eddy in her ability to thoroughly analyze, interpret, and logically expound the many vast and weighty questions with which she deals in her writings. Her style is simple and natural, and in her choice of words she shows an acute perception of the exact meaning she wishes to convey. There is almost a Biblical rhythm in some of her messages, an easy and metrical flow, which makes it exceedingly easy and attractive to read aloud. Her writings have stood the acid test of attacks from all grades and schools of critics, as has also her Christian character.

Her textbook is the inspiration and guide to millions of people today who are drinking deep of the healing draughts from this fountain of Truth and Love. They find this book good and helpful, not only in their time of physical needs, but also in their social, financial, and spiritual needs as well. They find that it is indeed the Key to the Scriptures, for it unlocks and makes plain to all who perceive her point of view, the deep things of God and man.

Is it any wonder, then, that people in all walks of life, are grateful to God for being healed and set free from the thraldom of evil of every kind through Christian Science? They are enabled to live a pure, happy, and prosperous life, because this woman of God was not only good enough but pure enough to receive this revelation from God, as well as wise enough to found and establish a church which is demonstrating to the world that it is lifting people out of all kinds of evil, and enabling all who abide by its Principle to live to God only, and triumph over evil through the realization of its truth.

Mrs. Eddy was not only inspired when she wrote the Christian Science textbook, but also when she wrote her other writings and her messages to her church as well, as is evidenced by the further fact that these messages of love also bring healing from sin and disease. *By their fruits ye shall know them,* said Jesus the Christ.

In 1866, Mrs. Eddy stood alone with God, poor in worldly goods, and not over rich in influential friends. But she waited on her dear heavenly Father, and He led her and directed her step by step, until she attained a position of pre-eminence in the world, and drew unto herself vast numbers of devoted and influential friends who deeply love and reverence her; but they do not worship her, as some claim. They love her for what she is and what she has done, and will continue to do for them and all the world.

Her followers are faithful students of the Bible. I am frank to say that in all my experience I have never come in contact with any other church whose members so uniformly and faithfully study both the Old and New Testaments, and do it because of their deep love for the Scriptures. The common testimony among Scientists is that the Bible became a new book to them after they became interested in Christian Science. When this blessed truth is once planted in a receptive mind it is there to stay. Sooner or later it will germinate and spring forth and bear fruit, *some thirtyfold, some sixty, and some an hundred.*

Mrs. Eddy further showed her unselfishness and deep love for all mankind when she bequeathed in her will the residue of her large estate to aid in the maintenance and spread of Christian Science throughout the whole world.

Her followers are deeply grateful to God for the fact that every institution and activity Mrs. Eddy established has proven a success, and of inestimable value in the unfoldment, protection, and spread of the Christ-Truth.

We had joined The Mother Church in June, 1901. The next June Mrs. Simonsen was invited to join the Normal class of the Metaphysical College, which was gratefully accepted and enjoyed more than words can express, and she, too, received her diploma, duly signed by Mrs. Eddy as president and Mr. Kimball as teacher.

After this visit to Pleasant View we were elected First Members of The Mother Church at the request of Mrs. Eddy.

E FINALLY returned to Brooklyn full of joy and thanksgiving to our dear heavenly Father for all of the good that had come to us, and for the better and higher understanding of God, man, and of the Discoverer of Christian Science. It seemed as though I had had a taste of how the disciples felt after their experience on the Mount of Transfiguration with our Master. I felt as though I could meet any problem with ease and assurance of success. And with it all I enjoyed such a clear and sweet sense of God's presence and power; but it was not long before I had to stand the supreme test of my understanding of God and Christian Science.

When we rented the house we were living in we took a lease from January, 1901, until October first, having a verbal agreement with the agent that if we so wished, we could renew our lease at the same rental for another year.

We had been home from Boston less than one week when we received notice from the agent that he would be unable to carry out his verbal agreement, as the house had been sold and the new owner wished to occupy it himself. There was nothing else for us to do but to find another house. After a careful search, we finally found one which seemed suitable for our large family, and well located for a practitioner's home. But the rental was six hundred and sixty dollars a year, which was considered a big rent in those days, and especially for one who had not yet made his financial demonstration. After working faithfully over the problem in Christian Science, we felt that it was our privilege to take it, knowing and realizing that God would provide for our every need.

When I took the house the agent said it would be three or four days before the lease would be ready for me to sign, as he would have to send it out of town to the owner for his signature first. I was thankful for this little interval, because I did not have all the necessary funds on hand to pay the first month's rent. But when the lease came back I had the money. God had provided it for me through my practice. Some may think I simply took a chance, but this is not true. I only went ahead and signed up for this new house after I was thoroughly convinced that it was the right thing for me to do.

We were soon moved and nicely settled in our new home, rejoicing in the forward step that we had taken. One week later I came to my office one morning, and on my desk was a letter addressed to me enclosing a check for fifty dollars. The letter stated it was from some of my friends in First Church of Christ, Scientist, Brooklyn, New York. Continuing, it read, "We deeply appreciate the noble stand you have taken for Christian Science, and what this means, not only to yourself, but to the Cause as well. If you will permit us we would love to be a party to your financial demonstration. We enclose a check for fifty dollars, and a like amount of fifty dollars will be forthcoming on the first day of each month until you have made your financial demonstration."

I cannot express in words the joy and gratitude that filled my heart as I read this little message of love. That evening when I showed it to my brave wife she wept for joy. But, somehow, that same evening it came to me that I should not accept this love offering. There was a higher demonstration for me to make. I thought and prayed over it to see if this were the voice of Truth or error, but the conviction became clearer and clearer that it was not for me to keep it.

The Crucial Test

When I told my good wife what had come to me, she said, "My dear, I cannot see why you can not keep this gift of love. You know these friends love you dearly and rejoice in doing this for you. Are you sure it is not error trying to push you out beyond your depth?" I assured her I deeply appreciated this generous gift, but as long as I felt as I did about it, I did not see how I could keep it conscientiously. I must above all things be obedient to God. Then she said, "Would it not be a great sense of relief to you to know that you had fifty dollars coming in the first of each month for a time? It would almost pay our house rent, and would not this be a help to you in your work?"

I told her it no doubt would be a sense of relief and a great help also, but as long as I felt that it was the leadings of the divine Mind, I must put it all on the altar and say, "Not my will, but Thine be done." "Well," she said, "you know best. Follow your highest understanding in the matter and you will be led to do the right thing. We will work over it faithfully and leave it all in the hands of God." This we did that night and the next day, but the conviction still remained with me that I should return the check.

The following day I did so, explaining my convictions to the good lady who had brought me the letter containing the check, further requesting her to tell my kind friends how I felt about the matter, and to thank them deeply for their love and great kindness to me and mine. In returning this check of fifty dollars, I also returned all future fifty dollar checks as well. I was enabled to do this gladly, however, and with perfect assurance and confidence in my heavenly Father's loving care of us all. I felt free and happy because I was divinely assured that I had done the right thing.

The end, however, was not yet. I still had to demonstrate and prove that my stand was correct. All went well until about one week before the first of the next month, when I realized that in a few days the rent for the house would become due, as well as the maid's wages. Up to this time my brave and devoted wife had done all the housework and taken care of the children as well. Noble girl. The long, cold, eastern winter was at the door and our little family needed suitable clothing, together with the warmth and protection a full coal bin, now empty, would afford.

The old serpent hissed and bared its fangs of fear, discouragement, despair, and failure, until I seemed to be in a dark dungeon, with evil beasts ready to devour me. The mental conflict lasted for three days and three nights. I felt, however, I could not turn to a single human being for aid, no, not even for counsel. I realized it was the crucial

testing time of my faith in God, and my understanding of God as my only source of substance and
supply. I realized, too, it was a most sacred hour
for me and I did not dare to look to the right or
the left, but unswervingly to my dear heavenly
Father, as did Daniel when he was in the lion's den.

By thus lovingly holding steadfastly and tenaciously to Principle, I gained a higher understanding of prayer, and a truer scientific understanding
of substance, and how to demonstrate it. I realized
that it was never in nor of matter, but always in
the unity of ever present good—God. Then Truth
and love dispelled the darkness and *there was light:*
and I realized that the demonstration was made.
From that hour God's rich and unlimited blessings
rested upon my labors for Him and suffering
humanity as I had never experienced before. I was
soon abundantly able to pay every bill, my accumu-
lated indebtedness, and supply my family with
everything needful more abundantly than ever
before. With heartfelt rejoicing I could say, *Let the
sea roar, and the fulness thereof: let the fields rejoice, and all that is therein. . . . O give thanks unto
the Lord; for he is good; for his mercy endureth
forever* (I Chron. 16:32, 34).

The thirty-seventh Psalm, which has been one
of my favorite Psalms since I was a boy of four-

teen, came to me with a fulness of joy which I had never before realized, especially verses 3-6: *Trust in the Lord, and do good; so shalt thou dwell in the land, and verily thou shalt be fed. . . . he shall give thee the desires of thine heart. Commit thy way unto the Lord; trust also in him; and he shall bring it to pass. And he shall bring forth thy right-eousness as the light, and thy judgment as the noonday.*

It was a year almost to the day from the time I wrote my resignation from the Methodist Episcopal Church and ministry, and all it included, that I made my financial demonstration. To me it was a year well spent, for the experience, liberty, free-dom, and joy that came with it is beyond anything I can describe, except in the words of Isaiah, *Thou wilt keep him in perfect peace, whose mind is stayed on thee: because he trusteth in thee. Trust ye in the Lord for ever: for in the Lord JEHOVAH is everlasting strength* (Isaiah 26:3, 4).

I related this experience to Judge Hanna, who was at that time First Reader of The Mother Church, and editor of *The Christian Science Journal* and *The Christian Science Sentinel,* when I called on him in Boston one day. After I had finished, he said: "Brother Simonsen, when you came to the place in your beautiful experience where these friends gave you fifty dollars, with an assurance that a like amount would be forthcoming on the first of each month until you had made your financial demonstration, I thought it was the most beautiful demonstration of its kind I had ever heard, and I did not see why you could not have kept this gift of love; but I can see now that you made a much higher demonstration by returning it, and demonstrating that God alone was your supply."

In telling my experience to another active Scientist, he said: "Mr. Simonsen, this experience of yours will be of untold value to many, many people who are striving to make their demonstration over the claims of lack and limitation." I have found this to be true.

It is because I realize the importance of this fact that I wish to share my rich and reassuring experience with all mankind, especially with those who are struggling with, and who are earnestly striving to demonstrate over, the false beliefs of lack and limitation. My earnest prayer and hope is that it may shed some helpful light on how to gain this understanding and realization of the Truth which brings man into his full birthright—abundance of all good. Jesus said, *"Seek ye first the kingdom* [understanding] *of God, and his righteousness; and all these things shall be added unto you.* (Matt. 6: 33).

It was not long after I had made my demonstration over lack and limitation that I was invited by First Church of Christ, Scientist, in New Haven, Conn., to become their First Reader. I accepted their invitation and we moved our little family to New Haven. Shortly after this Mrs. Simonsen was elected to the position of Second Reader, which she lovingly and successfully filled. We found it a great opportunity for doing good, and to bring this blessed message of Truth and Love to the many hungry hearts that came to the services. I shall long remember how one poor lady who had been almost totally deaf since she had an attack of scarlet fever when she was only one and a half years old, was beautifully healed of her deafness during the reading of the Bible and *Science and Health* at one of the Wednesday evening testimonial meetings.

In the early days of Christian Science, and for some time after, it was not an unusual thing for articles derogatory to Christian Science, and to Mrs. Eddy and her followers to appear in the public press, and it became necessary to appoint a Publication Committee with headquarters in Boston, Mass., with assistant Publication Committees in every state and country where Christian Science was established, in order to promptly and lovingly correct all such erroneous reports.

Shortly after I had settled in New Haven, I was appointed the assistant Publication Committee for the State of Connecticut. This was a most interesting work.

When I first took up this important work, a friend took me around to the newspaper officials and introduced me as the new assistant Publication Committee for the State of Connecticut; but I was hardly greeted with common courtesy. This condition of things, however, quickly changed, and it was not long before the editors were pleased to receive me and my corrections of erroneous statements concerning Christian Science which had appeared in their respective papers.

During my second year of service in this capacity things had changed so radically that some of the editors asked me if I would contribute articles to their paper concerning Christian Science. They said they found the interest in this new movement had become so great that the people demanded more information about this interesting subject.

I gladly accepted their invitations and thereafter contributed many articles to the several papers.

The wife of the editor of the New Haven *Leader*, who was one of the special writers for this paper, interviewed me one day and wrote a lengthy and impartial article relating in detail my life and experiences much as has been written in the preceding chapters.

The manner in which she handled her topic created not only much favorable comment, but it awakened many, because of their fair sense and love of justice, to take up the study of Christian Science.

The result of her interview published in *The Leader,* and later republished in *The Christian Science Sentinel,* is as follows:

THE ETHICS OF CHRISTIAN SCIENCE

———

Discussed by an Unbeliever Who Does,
However, Believe in the Ethics
of Justice.

———

First Church of Christ, Scientist, of New Haven, is congratulating itself on the acceptance of a call extended to the Rev. Mr. Simonsen of Brooklyn, who has already commenced his new duties as First Reader of the little band of believers of this faith who have their meeting place on the second floor of the building at 156 Orange Street.

Mr. Simonsen is making arrangements to bring his wife and seven children to this city immediately, and it was during a few minutes' respite in house hunting that I met and talked with this new comer to the city, at the request of one of the members of his flock. Mr. Simonsen's name will suggest to those who keep in close touch with currents events along all lines, the great sensation in the Methodist denomination of the country which his coming out for Christian Science created more than a year ago.

Through the press, and Dr. Buckley, editor of the *Christain Advocate,* one version at least of the story was pretty thoroughly circulated.

I listened to Mr. Simonsen's calm, unimpassioned statement of how, after being educated for a Methodist minister and preaching the gospel of this denomination for many years, he was finally compelled, for the faith that was in him, to forsake all he had achieved in reputation and prosperity and begin life all over again and this from an entirely new doctrinal standpoint.

Among many things related by Mr. Simonsen, he told of early lack of sympathy with the beliefs of Christian Science, and that at the start no more hopeless subject to have worked upon could have existed than he.

Fifteen years ago last summer he was taken very ill of a complication of ailments and several physicians had apparently exhausted their skill in treating him without avail.

A friend called one day and being somewhat interested in Christian Science suggested as a last hope that the sick man try it, saying, "It cannot hurt you and may possibly help."

Having given up all hope of help through the accepted medical channels, the minister finally consented to see a Christian Scientist, and in seventeen treatments was made well again. Even then, he could not accept the theology of this new faith—as its followers claim it to be—nor bring his mind to surrender all the beliefs and plans of a lifetime and come out for Christian Science.

As the years passed he read, studied, and thought on the subject, attended classes, and became able to heal the sick; but never during those years of uncertainty, he maintains, did he ever try to impress his growing belief on the members of his flock or discuss it deeply with any of them. His healing powers were confined to his own family and a few outside his congregation.

Some of his children have never tasted medicine.

The climax came a year ago last summer, when one of his children had a disease which refused to yield to his treatment and he was forced either to go to a physician or a healer. He chose the latter, who on hearing his errand, asked him the following searching questions: "Why do you, a Christian minister, come to me for healing? Do you carry out the divine command, 'Heal the sick'? or if not, why does not the church to which you belong practice the healing taught in the New Testament?" and last of all "Do you expect to get the benefit of Christian Science healing for your child, when you are not willing to acknowledge what it has done for you and yours?" These were hard questions to answer and they stirred up a fresh struggle in the heart of this minister on whose face is stamped honesty of purpose, and in whose voice it speaks.

It meant a great deal to this man established for years over a prosperous Brooklyn church, domiciled in a beautiful parsonage home, with a large family to take thought for. This was the human, the material side of the question, and who shall condemn, if it weighed heavily on his mind in making his final decision.

Once more he read the Science literature, searching for light, for Truth, determined he would either find it or surrender it and be at peace one way or the other. He was finally enabled to say, "The Lord will take care of my family if I honestly believe my path leads this way," and at last the full fledged decision was made to face the ridicule of the world, uproot himself from his comfortable position, and announce himself as a firm believer in the tenets of Christian Science.

This he did at the quarterly conference in the fall of 1900, and while the members were surprised and naturally sorry, they still believed in their brother and stood loyally by him, those of his church urging him to remain with them, even though he believed as he did. The minister replied, "When you hear what the world says, you will not want me." But even this did not daunt some of his staunch friends, who shook their heads, firm as was Peter of old, in their belief in their own unchangeableness.

Knowing very well that he could not be a good Methodist minister on one side and a Christian Scientist on the other, Mr. Simonsen asked for his release, and on the last Sunday of the last year of the nineteenth century he preached his farewell sermon to the congregation he had served faithfully for so many years.

Some of his parishioners attested to their continued friendship and esteem by presenting him with a handsome parting gift. But the incident was not yet closed, for at the next meeting of the conference, the question of returning Mr. Simonsen's credentials, which he had placed in their hands according to custom, was brought up and the motion was made, discussed, and passed that they be returned. This action was accompanied by complimentary remarks on the pastor's work among them. Soon after the vote had been taken, Dr. Buckley arrived, and learning what had transpired took the floor and said they had no right to give Mr. Simonsen these credentials, for he was not going to minister to a Christian people, or words to that effect.

The debate became spirited, the editor firm in his own belief, no doubt, that he was acting in the interests of the Christian religion, refusing to be convinced, and finally getting the motion rescinded and another one before the meeting. His stronger personality and persistency combined finally triumphed, and the broad-minded, tolerant action of the meeting was supplanted by one inspired more by human prejudice than the true essence of the Christian religion. "And did the Lord provide, Mr. Simonsen?" inquired the attentive listener. "Yes," answered the man who had surrendered much for his faith's sake. "Neither my family nor myself have wanted for the comforts of life since we left our beautiful parsonage home, with its elegant furnishings and betook ourselves to hired apartments, where we did not know where the next dollar was coming from." "And you have never regretted it?" "Not for an instant. Had I the same path to travel again, I should make the same choice and my wife is in full sympathy with me." "And in what manner, if I may inquire, did the Lord provide, Mr. Simonsen?" The pleasant smile which is easily won played over the new First Reader's face as he made reply: "I have been healing the sick in Brooklyn the past year and have been remarkably successful in my work." He then gave several illustrations in support of his statement, so calmly, firmly, truthfully related, that it fairly staggers one's unbelief. It is one thing to read of these in print, together with the ironical comments that usually accompany them. It is another to hear them from the lips of educated, honest men and women, who say, "I know these things are true, because I have seen them or I have experienced them," and such opportunities have come to me a possible dozen times. Therefore, it seems worse than foolish to treat the belief with contempt and say, "Because I do not understand it, it is not so." That method strikes at the very foundation of all progress in science, art, and religion.

If we tolerated nothing but what we could fully understand, even in the natural world, we should have to surrender many wonderful modern inventions.

The wireless telegraphy, the telephone, the trolley, the thousand and one wonders of modern times could only be explained as miracles to our ancestors of a hundred years ago, could they revisit the earth.

Who shall say, "I know it is not so because I cannot understand it," that divine Power has ceased to act in a definite and (to us) material way, but to the Christian Scientist in the natural way, through the spirit which they claim should dominate and control the body.

That men like Mr. Simonsen, after long thought and study, are finally impelled to accept this doctrine, which is certainly a beautiful one ethically, if not practical scientifically, must needs "give us pause" before the whole subject is characterized as a "fad," and its followers as "cranks." RHEA.

In *The Evening Leader,* New Haven, Conn.

I shall ever be deeply grateful to my dear heavenly Father for that night when I sat in the Primary Class, twenty-seven years ago, and became conscious of the dawning light of this higher understanding and a crystalizing realization of the great truth, set forth in Christian Science, that the same Principle which heals sin, heals sickness, poverty, want, and woe as well. I recognized it was the one and only panacea.

As I progressed in my study, practice, and understanding of this omnipotent Principle, the vision of what God's salvation to all mankind really and truly included, became marvelous in its portrayal of God's great love for His children.

From that first night in class, I began to put this new yet old eternal Truth, as set forth by its Discoverer and Founder, into daily practice, not only for my own and my family's good, but also for the good of suffering humanity as well; more earnestly even, than with my former understanding of God's proffered salvation from sin as generally accepted. I say, generally accepted, because I know, as well as any deep-thinking Christian will, and does acknowledge, that the so-called orthodox religion does not include in any definite or scientific manner, deliverance from aught but its followers' sins and a guilty conscience, thus endowing them with an ability to love God commensurate only to their understanding of Him. But the Bible, Christian Science, and my own experience in demonstrating the Principle underlying this full and complete salvation, show me that this is only a partial, not the grand and full salvation provided by God, from all eternity, for all the ills that human flesh is heir to.

In addition thereto, I have found that Christian Science also reveals to all mankind the eternal Principle underlying this full and complete salvation and furthermore, how all may successfully apply this Principle to their every human need, if they will only seek and gain the correct understanding of God, and obey Him as they do the principle of mathematics.

Ever since I came into this blessed understanding of my God, and have proven the ability of this Principle to heal and save from all human woes, the great longing of my heart has been, and is so daily, to help mankind to see this omnipresent light.

For the good that has been and is now my experience in seeking and reaping the peace, joy, and abundance the demonstration of this divine Principle of all true existence supplies, is the light or true understanding that I so earnestly desire to pass on to my fellow man, for by so doing, the Scriptural command of Jesus the Christ to *Let your light* [understanding] *so shine before men, that they may see your good works* [demonstrations], *and glorify your Father which is in heaven* (Matt. 5:16), is in part fulfilled through the happiness this omnipotent and omnipresent Truth can, will, and does express in every one who will earnestly seek, practice, and obey this divine law.

I do not believe it is possible for any man or woman who has tested, through experience, the joy, peace, and calm trust, the understanding his eternal birthright embraces of the allness of good and the limitless abundance of substance and supply, not to earnestly long for the opportunity to have others also possess it and share with him this never-ending source from which to draw.

For this reason, and for no other, has it been my purpose to present to my brethren my experience and proofs of our heavenly Father's omnipresent love, care and supply, gained through the study, practice, and demonstration of Christian Science.

In a world darkened by the seeming power of evil, with a misconception and misunderstanding of man as God's image and likeness, and with humanity struggling for the good which—if they would only seek in the way God has decreed for all time,—is theirs by only complying with His loving demands, it is a joyful task to cry with Isaiah (55:1), *Ho, every one that thirsteth, come ye to the waters, and he that hath no money; come ye, buy, and eat; yea, come, buy wine and milk without money and without price.*

CHAPTER X

REALIZATION OF TRUTH

Stop looking at your bank account. Know that the one and only bank is God's bank, and that has never been, is not now, and never can be closed to God's idea. It is ever operative in your behalf, and you can draw on it morning, noon and night to the extent of your REALIZATION OF THE TRUTH: and you will find it will meet your every human need. It is all there waiting for you, just the same as the answer to your mathematical problems is there waiting for you to realize it.

"The silver is mine, and the gold is mine, saith the Lord of hosts." (Haggai 2:8)

CHAPTER XII

THE BIBLICAL BASIS OF DEMONSTRATING SUBSTANCE AND SUPPLY

OME time after I had taken my stand publicly for Christian Science, and had passed successfully through the most crucial test of my whole life, namely, that of demonstrating over lack and limitation and proving that God was my supply, I visited Boston and attended a testimonial meeting in the Mother Church, The First Church of Christ, Scientist.

In giving my own testimony that evening, I related some of my experiences in coming into Christian Science, as well as my demonstration of the abundance of supply according to the Principle of divine Science. At the close of the meeting, and the next day, a number of Christian Scientists came to me and said, "Mr. Simonsen, tell me please, how did you do it?"

They went on to explain, as hundreds have done since that day, saying, "We can successfully apply the Principle of Christian Science to the healing of sin and disease, but when it comes to healing the belief of lack and limitation, and demonstrating substance, we fail."

From that day, and daily ever since, I have heard this human cry—"Mr. Simonsen, tell me please, how did you do it? How can I reach this same understanding of the Principle of Christian Science, that I, too, may destroy my belief of lack and limitation, and demonstrate the abundance of good?"

I endeavored then, and have faithfully labored ever since, to help each honest seeker into this understanding of the infinite supply or allness of good, and how to gain it for themselves; for I know from my own personal experience what it means to be in ignorance of our birthright as a child of God, on the one hand, and the peace, joy, liberty, supply, and boundless bliss that the understanding of God and our real or actual birthright brings to us, on the other hand.

This message of love, and especially this chapter on demonstrating substance and supply, is the fruition of my life-long study of the Scriptures and the application of the Principle underlying the teachings set forth in Christian Science, for the last forty-one years, together with my daily study of patients in hand and their particular needs in the line of substance and supply, calling for a careful and prayerful analysis of the many forms of error attacking each individual, and how to successfully meet and master these erroneous claims in Truth.

The reader must understand and realize that a careless perusal of this chapter without thoughtful pondering of its contents, may eliminate the very good I so earnestly desire him to gain, the real helpfulness I desire to impart, which is the main reason for publishing this volume and revealing my own sacred experience to the world.

Slow, thoughtful study—with calm reasoning, the application of its message to the reader's belief in his own sense of this seeming problem of lack and limitation, will, I am sure, produce for him an entirely different and joyous aspect of life, and an understanding of his birthright; he will also find his journey illumined and made more glorious and radiant for God and mankind through the realization that God, Spirit, is the only substance and supply—always at hand, always available—the fulness of ever-present Love.

The same Principle, I have found by experience, which heals the sick and the sinning, heals also every and all manner of diseased financial and business conditions; for this more comprehensive understanding of God and His relationship to all His children, brings substance and supply into its true light where each and everyone may see, grasp, and utilize it.

Until this fuller and, to me, higher understanding of the Scriptures and of Christian Science is gained, one may demonstrate substance and supply now and then; but it will be found to be more of a hit-or-miss process, as when some Christians recover from sickness through prayer based upon and springing from blind faith.

In my extended study of the Bible, sacred history, and *Science and Health with Key to the Scriptures* I have learned that it is sin, ignorance, and a misconception of God and of man's own birthright— the supply of all good and his dominion over all the earth—that has plunged him into this seething and foaming abyss of human misery—fear, lack and limitation, want and woe, despair and untold suffering.

God declared through his prophet Jeremiah, *Your iniquities have turned away these things, and your sins have withholden good things from you.* Also through Isaiah He states, *Behold, the Lord's hand is not shortened, that it cannot save; neither his ear heavy, that it cannot hear: But your iniquities have separated between you and your God, and your sins have hid his face from you, that he will not hear.*

God complains of this ignorance of Himself when in Isaiah He declares, *The ox knoweth his owner, and the ass his Master's crib: but Israel doth not know, my people doth not consider.* And again, in the writings of Jeremiah he states it thus: *Yea, the stork in the heaven knoweth her appointed times; and the turtle and the crane and the swallow observe the time of their coming; but my people know not the judgment of the Lord.* Jesus complained of this ignorance, as did Paul. Jesus said, *Ye do err, not knowing the Scriptures* (Matthew 22:29). Also in the midst of his suffering on the cross Jesus brought out this lamentable condition of man in his appeal to the heavenly Father in these memorable words: *Father, forgive them; for they know not what they do* (Luke 23:34).

St. Paul portrayed this pitiable condition of man as spending his time in the vanity of his own human, carnal or mortal mind thus: *Having the understanding darkened, being alienated from the life of God through the ignorance that is in them, because of the blindness of their heart* [mind] (Ephesians 4:18). *Because the carnal mind is enmity against God: for it is not subject to the law of God, neither indeed can be* (Romans 8:7).

The rejection of the so-called human, carnal or mortal mind of man as having entity, and the acceptance of all mentality as being God, the one and only Mind, and that one infinite, of which man (all men) are but the reflective idea, is the first requirement of every one who desires to acquire a true understanding of the Principle of all that exists. Even the beginner, in his acceptance of Christian Science, does not grasp in its entirety the clarity of so antipodal an understanding to that of the world's concept of and tenacious holding to the belief of many minds. Yet the whole structure of man's understanding, and his opportunity to ever demonstrate his oneness with God and all good, which from the foundation of creation has been his birthright, must unequivocally be the first and foremost step taken in his pathway back to the realization of his relationship to God, and freedom from the woes of materiality. For *the natural* [carnal or mortal minded] *man receiveth not the things of the Spirit* [Mind] *of God: for they are foolishness unto him: neither can he know them, because they are spiritually* [mentally] *discerned* (I Cor. 2:14). *For to be carnally minded is death; but to be spiritually minded is life and peace* (Romans 8:6).

The foregoing quotations are some of God's admonitions concerning man's ignorance and continual refusal to understand and accept his true relationship with his heavenly Father, which has separated him from and blinded him to the infinite good that is ever with him—a blindness that has caused all the human woe, bloodshed, suffering, and unrighteous living which the world's history records all down the ages.

It is absolutely imperative that man's ignorance of God, and of all the good He has provided for the benefit of man, be dispelled, and mankind set free from this long bondage to evil.

In dispelling the ignorance of man's relationship to God and His supply of all good, I find the result depends upon mankind's willingness to awaken from his ignorance and slothfulness, and comply with the simple and reasonable conditions laid down by our heavenly Father, omnipotent Mind, for the realization of his God-given birthright—the possession of all good, and liberty from any and every limitation whatsoever,—as well as his freedom from all past sins, no matter how vile or degrading, and believed to be beyond the hope of forgiveness.

The Bible is replete with offers of full and free salvation, clearly demonstrating that God does not leave man out in the wilderness of his sinful condition, hopeless and without a Saviour, for in the first chapter of Isaiah as proof thereof, we read: *Come now, and let us reason together, saith the Lord: though your sins be as scarlet, they shall be as white as snow; though they be red like crimson, they shall be as wool. If ye be willing and obedi-*

ent, ye shall eat the good of the land. Again, in the eighty-fourth Psalm we read: *For the Lord God is a sun and shield: the Lord will give grace and glory: no good thing will he withhold from them that walk uprightly. O Lord of hosts, blessed is the man that trusteth in thee.*

Error, or the one evil, seems to realize that it cannot forever keep man in the awful mental darkness of the past, nor from understanding something of the full salvation God has provided for him through Christ; therefore it makes a desperate effort to keep him from the understanding of true substance—the essence of existence and true spiritual worship—by holding him tenaciously in the false belief that man's life, health, strength, sustenance, protection, comfort, happiness, joy, and pleasure depend upon matter and this erroneous substance which Paul called "filthy lucre."

Man's intense holding to, and his adamant belief in the power of material money as substance, has made money "the god of this world," and he seemingly willing to make the utmost sacrifice for his false conception of substance, thereby binding himself hand and foot to this false god. Thus we see how evil has succeeded in mesmerizing mankind into the false and disastrous belief that man can and does exist in and on matter, and apart from God—that material money is substance. Furthermore, evil has struck its main blow at the very foundation of man's existence and true spiritual worship, causing him to believe in the actuality of matter and material money as substance, thus violating the First Commandment, *Thou shalt have no other gods before me* (Exodus 20:3).

This belief, blindly accepted so universally, has in turn established another false and disastrous belief that man has fallen and has separated himself from God, which both the Bible (when correctly understood) and Christian Science repudiate, because the real man in the image and likeness of God could never be separated from the eternal I AM; neither could the Almighty be robbed of His own image and likeness.

This universally believed-in or Adam man, i.e., the sensuous, corporeal concept, flesh and bones, born of woman, is not the image or Godlikeness, but is the result of believing in matter as substance, and the sensuous, mortal concept of man as a creator of man. The Godlike, or image and likeness, is the individual consciousness of man (all men), free from material concepts, so-called material laws, and reflecting or manifesting all and only the creations of God, Mind, the one and only consciousness; pure, undefiled, and defined by St. John (I John 3:9) thus: *Whosoever is born* [begotten] *of*

God doth not commit sin [believe in matter as substance, and as having power either for good or evil]; *for his seed* [Godlike consciousness] *remaineth in him: and he cannot sin, because he is born* [begotten] *of God.* Therefore the mortal or material man is not the real man, nor has he fallen, for he has never been the man of God's creating. He exists only in a supposititious human consciousness, a consciousness which has accepted matter as real. Neither is this human consciousness a reality, for it is not begotten [or born] of God.

It has ever been since evil was accepted by mortal man as true, and will so continue to be evil's superdevilish effort to blind man to his true, real, spiritual self, his eternal Godlikeness as image, and God as his only substance and supply, holding him as long as evil's falsity is believed in, to this false and misleading belief that there is substance matter, that material money is substance, and that he must have this substance at all costs or he will never be happy, contented, and prosperous; yea, that he is wholly and absolutely dependent upon it in every way, at all times, and under all circumstances and conditions.

If we will but carefully and correctly analyze the machinations of evil, we shall find that evil works through the reversal of Truth, that it begins this line of endeavor with man not only at his birth, and continues to do so until he passes on, but it exerts its evil schemes to capture and hold man as its bond-man before he is ever born. For evil starts its subtle and malicious attack with the tender, loving, and devoted mother before she has given birth to her child, by often causing her to fear and worry over sufficient money—"the filthy lucre"—for the care, support, education, etc., of her offspring; and perhaps for a successful entrance into a useful and worthy career.

Through this prenatal, mesmeric influence the offspring starts out on its unknown career handicapped, to sense, from the very beginning of mortal existence. It is often the case, too, that error tries to grip the child in this falsity through other members of the family, through relations, friends, neighbors, or enemies, and through the misleading public false and fixed idea or belief about the substance and supply of man.

Evil seems to make use of this false belief to the fullest extent, in order to keep man from coming into the correct understanding and realization of what his true substance and supply really is, the only place where it can be found, and how it may be obtained by every man, woman, and child who seek it, thus causing man to believe in, hold to, and lean upon matter and material things as substance, and reversing thereby the truth concerning God's care of man, and man's true substance and supply. To destroy this fallacy man must awaken out of such mesmeric mental miasma, and reverse his thinking, understanding, and realization of what is his true substance and supply.

It is true that man cannot get along without substance in the form of money; but be it always remembered that this substance and supply which man needs and is dependent upon for his existence, sustenance, protection, education, success, and happiness is not the false material substance called money or "fifthy lucre," but is the true spiritual idea of substance of which the material money is but the symbol, as we shall clearly see later on.

I have further discovered, and it cannot be too strongly emphasized, that when a man undertakes, through the correct understanding of the Scriptures and Christian Science, to demonstrate that God is the only substance, and that God actually is his one and only source of supply, he is striking at the very citadel of error—"the god of this world." Neither must he be surprised that the road is straight and narrow which leads to the understanding and realization that God is his only substance.

This mental struggle may become, and no doubt will be, the greatest of all his encounters with evil, for he must now prove to himself and to the world the utter falsity of the erroneous and misleading belief that material money is substance, and that he cannot exist without it.

This is the falsity which would try to force man to doubt God's goodness, to forget the all-sufficiency of Spirit to supply him with everything needful, and to cause him to believe that he can neither exist, although God is the life of man, proof positive that man's life is not in any way dependent upon matter, but wholly upon Spirit; nor be fed, although Christ said he was the bread of life; nor again, be clothed, although Jesus counselled them in the Sermon on the Mount when he said: *And why take ye thought for raiment? Consider the lilies of the field, how they grow; they toil not, neither do they spin: And yet I say unto you, That even Solomon in all his glory was not arrayed like one of these. Wherefore, if God so clothe the grass of the field . . . shall he not much more clothe you, O ye of little faith?*

This persistent falsity enters forcefully into the business world, suggesting man's inability to a success therein without its aid, when all business is God's business and always successful.

It strikes at man's support of charities and church in defiance of God's commanded blessing upon the man who careth for his unfortunate brother, as well as for the cause of Christ, promising as a reward, to open *the windows of heaven, and pour . . . out a blessing, that there shall not be room enough to receive it* (Mal. 3:10).

Again, it includes in its claim the freedom and the health of man in the face of Christ's eternal promise, that if man will but know and realize the truth, he shall be free: and as to the health of man, does not God declare through the prophets, and in the Psalms especially, does not David sing of God *who is the health of my countenance* [spiritually, man's whole being]?

Furthermore, the falsity insists that man cannot provide a home for himself and loved ones without the material money; yet Paul says, man hath *a building of God, an house, not made with hands, eternal in the heavens* [harmony:] not a home in the hereafter only, but now; for home is the abiding place of God's image or idea, man, provided by God with every lesser idea making for harmony, as we shall shortly note.

The Scriptures are literally full of God's commands to man to live a happy and joyous life, with no reference whatsoever that material money is a necessary concomitant and is the substance needed to bring about the blissful existence with which man's birthright as God's child—His image—endows him.

Herewith is one of the commands of God to man: *Go your way, eat the fat, and drink the sweet, . . . neither be ye sorry; for the joy of the Lord is your strength* (Neh. 8:10). And again note the fulness and completeness wherein God proclaims joy, freedom, and supply of all that pertains to man's existence and well-being, and His delight therein: *But be ye glad and rejoice for ever in that which I create: for, behold, I create Jerusalem* [harmony] *a rejoicing, and her people a joy. And I will rejoice in Jerusalem, and joy in my people: . . . And they shall build houses, and inhabit them; and they shall plant vineyards, and eat the fruit of them. . . . And it shall come to pass, that before they call, I will answer; and while they are yet speaking, I will hear* (Isaiah 65:18-24); clearly a statement that God, and not material money, is the substance and supply of man, providing for every need.

Jesus and Paul both strongly repudiated such a suggestion. Jesus, when being tempted to look to matter to supply his need, destroyed and showed how to destroy the lie by affirming, *Man shall not live by bread alone, but by every word that proceedeth out of the mouth of God.* Again, when requested by his disciples to eat, he stated, *I have meat to eat that ye know not of.* Paul affirmed the truth by declaring, *I can do all things through Christ which strengtheneth me;* not through material money.

There seems to be such a vague, generally misleading and incorrect idea of what substance really is—the human mind is so prone to believe that matter and material money are substance—that it becomes necessary for us, before we go deeply into the subject, to take up the definition of substance.

There is no word in any language, when studying spiritual truths, that needs to be so clearly understood as the word, substance. The world's concept and usage of the word, substance, is far from the spiritual reality embodied in its definition.

Webster defines substance as follows: "That which underlies all outward manifestation; substratum; the permanent spirit or cause of phenomena, whether material or spiritual; that which is real in distinction to that which is apparent; that which constitutes anything what it is. THE ESSENCE; that which makes a thing what it is, or gives it its essential nature; that in which qualities and attributes exist."

In writing to the Corinthians Paul sums it up in these words: *While we look not at the things which are seen, but at the things which are not*

*seen: for the things which are seen are temporal;
but the things which are not seen are eternal . . .
(For we walk by faith, not by sight).*

The author of Hebrews declares, *Now faith is
the substance* [that which underlies all outward
manifestation—Webster] *of things hoped for, the
evidence of things not seen;* that is, the recognition,
assurance, conviction and realization of the spiritual realities symbolized by material ideas.

From the foregoing definition of substance by
Webster, and Paul's positive assertion, it is self-
evident that God is the substance of every true and
right idea. Naturally there are grades of ideas, and
man is fully defined in Genesis as being the highest
idea of God, in fact, made in His image and likeness, reflecting the dominion and power of God.
Therefore man includes in himself all other right
ideas because he reflects the infinite Mind, the
Creator of all, in whom all things exist, consequently the substance of all.

Referring again to Webster, we find that one of
the definitions of idea is, "an embodiment of the
essential value or character of something; the typi-
cal quality which exists in the individual thing and
makes it symbolic of analogous things or concep-
tions." And of symbols, the same authority defines
the word as follows: "That which stands for and

represents something else; a visible sign or representation of an idea of quality; an emblem."

Both the Old and New Testaments abound in symbols that clearly establish this fact; and the truth applies not only to what man would call higher and greater ideas, but it is also set forth symbolically by means of the most humble and commonplace material things as well. For instance: God, through His prophet Malachi in the Old Testament, used material objects to set forth the spiritual idea of purifying and cleansing when the prophet wrote: *But who may abide the day of his coming? . . . for he is like a refiner's fire, and like fuller's soap: And he shall sit as a refiner and purifier of silver: . . . and purge them as gold and silver* (Malachi 3:2, 3).

The teachings of Christ and of his Apostles abound in many such symbolical illustrations. Jesus the Christ used "the rock" as the symbol of the spiritual foundation of his church (Matt. 16:18). He also used "the door" to illustrate the entrance into the understanding of his kingdom, and the opportunities for usefulness. Again, Jesus used "the vine and the branches" as symbolizing the idea of Christ (the Truth), and man's intimate and eternal oneness with God, the Principle of his being. On another occasion he used bread to illustrate and point to the spiritual idea back of it—"the bread of life."

St. Paul made use of even the cruel, material instruments of war to illustrate the spiritual preparedness and warfare for the overcoming and destruction of evil when he said: *Wherefore take unto you the whole armour of God, that ye may be able to withstand in the evil day, . . . having your loins girt about with truth, and having on the breastplate of righteousness; And your feet shod with the preparation of the gospel of peace; Above all, taking the shield of faith, . . . the helmet of salvation, and the sword of the Spirit, which is the word of God* (Ephesians 6:13-17).

St. John also went to a profound depth in his usage and interpretation, through material symbols, of the higher and loftier spiritual ideas. He brought out with marked clarity the "pure . . . water of life" by the material water. By the aid of the throne, he typified the power and dominion of "God and the Lamb." In the city of Jerusalem he found the symbol of the "New Jerusalem," "whose builder and maker is God," and, "that lieth four-square."

In fact every good object or right idea in the material creation symbolizes or alludes to a spiritual idea back of it. *For the invisible things of him from the creation of the world are clearly seen, being understood by the things that are made, even his eternal power and Godhead* (Romans 1:20).

In the solar system we find the sun, moon, and stars are often used as symbols of higher spiritual ideas: for instance, in speaking of the sun of righteousness and the healing power of Truth, Malachi says (Chap. 4:2), *But unto you that fear my name shall the Sun of righteousness arise with healing in his wings. In Revelation* (Chap. 22:16), "the bright and morning star" is used as a symbol of Christ, Truth.

From the preceding illustrations we are enabled to take up the subject, money, and examine and realize that the symbol, money, is the highest idea of an exchange between men and nations—an appreciation for a commodity needed or desired; or honesty, justice, and righteousness expressed in the appreciation of another's effort in our behalf; the true and spiritual embodiment in the give and take of brotherly love, or Christ's command of *Do unto others as you would have them do unto you.*

Inasmuch as the idea, money—not the material money, "the god of this world"—embodies the essential nature, character, and quality of honesty, justice, righteousness, appreciation, etc., all being attributes of God, we rightfully conclude that the material symbol of money is emblematic of real or spiritual substance, that is, the God qualities we have enumerated as attributes of God. Moreover, it is God expressed or manifested where and when the substance of money is needed to meet the human sense of need, and as such, man is never without substance, neither has he been, is not now, nor ever can be separated from it; for God is the omnipresent substance and supply of every needful idea to His own reflected image, man.

A clear example of the right usage of money, together with the understanding of the spiritual idea or reality back of the material symbol, is found in the twenty-second chapter of Matthew wherein the Pharisees sought to entangle Jesus concerning the payment of tribute money unto Caesar.

Jesus, you are aware, demanded to know whose image and superscription were on the coin, and on their reply that they were Caesar's, Jesus gave his forceful statement: *Render therefore unto Caesar the things which are Caesar's; and unto God the things that are God's.* Herein Jesus was showing them to deal justly, honestly, righteously, and in all brotherly kindness and appreciation with Caesar, inasmuch as these were Godlike spiritual qualities with which the man of God's creating, and in God's own image and likeness, is constantly supplied.

The usage of the symbol—material money—was the act of paying to Caesar that which was Caesar's; and because man expresses, reflects, or manifests these Godlike qualities or attributes we have mentioned, it was God, Mind, then, which supplied man with the symbol or emblem with which to manifest these qualities. They were, in other words, to acknowledge God and His never-failing spiritual qualities, which in turn would supply the symbol that made possible rendering unto Caesar that which was Caesar's.

Many good Christians are prone to look upon money as "filthy lucre" only, and not as a spiritual idea of God, Mind, which makes possible the expressing and fulfilling of the exchange we have mentioned. But if one will closely note Paul's assertion that it was the "love of money"—material money, "the god of this world"—that was wrong, and not the idea of honesty of purpose that money stands for, the reader will grasp the understanding of the true idea of money, and God as the substance of it.

Among the many strong and startling statements not only made by Mrs. Eddy in her writings, but which she, as well, abundantly demonstrated and proved without any doubt whatsoever, was her teaching concerning the immutable fact that God is the substance of every good and right idea, be it in the form of man or money, not the material sense, but the spiritual idea back of both man and money as simply a manifestation of God Himself. Through this discovery it becomes clear and understandable how God can really be and is All-in-all, yea, is ALL.

The false and misleading conception concerning matter and material substance and supply, was universally held by rich and poor alike, until Mrs. Eddy, through her clear and logical teaching on this all important subject, true substance, startled the world out of the mesmeric falsity concerning the truth about every right idea. This fundamental truth she brought to light, has caused many to become awakened to their need of a more thorough discernment and rectification of their former beliefs concerning matter and material money as their substance and supply, and of the bondage under which such beliefs had heretofore placed them.

It has furthermore destroyed their former reliance on the material, and has corrected their thinking to an understanding wherein to demonstrate the fulness of God's blessings to man, an undertaking sought not through their own thinking, searching, and laboring in the so-called material realm, but by their seeking God that Spirit may reveal what substance is.

In seeking God and His spiritual supply, one must realize it is not the material money nor its supposed power to relieve our needs that we are seeking, but that we may truthfully manifest the God-idea of brotherly love, honesty, justice, righteousness, and an appreciation of another's effort in our behalf, which comprise true spiritual value, and are in reality spiritual attributes.

Nothing can stop the inflow to, nor the manifestation of this right idea of money by man, God's image, when he truly understands substance and supply correctly and realizes that it is his birthright, yea, duty as a child of the great I AM, to reflect here and now the eternal idea or essence of that which money exemplifies.

I have learned that we must make nothing substance apart from God, for there is none else; therefore there can be nothing apart from the infinite ALL. Consequently you cannot separate supply, substance, the true idea of money, from Mind; for God is All-in-all. If you have God you also have all substance and supply in abundance, just as you have life, health, joy, peace, love, etc., in abundance. There cannot be any real something apart from the infinite ALL. Nor can it be limited. It must be as full and infinite as the infinite Mind itself.

Therefore, when man looks to matter and makes material money his substance, he departs from the straight and narrow way and finds himself wandering hopelessly in the wilderness of illusions, thus bringing upon himself the dire consequences of departing from the one God.

Through this correct view of money and substance, I have found that it lifts man out of the sordid and limited sense which material money places on him when he becomes a slave to it. Truth lifts him into the understanding of God, Principle, as All-in-all; and furthermore, it lifts him into the realization of his God-given birthright—the allness of good.

I have also found that when man gains this, his birthright, he gains his true liberty, freedom, power, and dominion, and begins to live and enjoy life as God has planned for man from all eternity; furthermore he finds himself becoming more helpful to mankind. This true and correct understanding—realizing God as his substance and supply—causes man to lose his sense of envy, jealousy, covetousness, etc., because man will then see and realize that the supply of all good is as infinite as God Himself, and therefore there is an infinite supply for each and every one who will abandon leaning on matter as substance, and enter into his God-given birthright.

I find that all through the Scriptures God emphasizes the fact that evil originates, unfolds, and proceeds from the human or mortal mind. Throughout the sacred writings it speaks in various and sundry places of "a man's heart," meaning thereby, his mind, and the thoughts proceeding from his heart or mind.

In the sixth chapter of Genesis, we read, *And God saw that the wickedness of man was great in the earth, and that every imagination of the thoughts of his heart* [mind] *was only evil continually.* Jesus said: *Wherefore think ye evil in your hearts*" [minds] (Matt. 9:4)?

Again, in the seventh chapter of Mark, we note that Jesus taught them, saying, . . . *out of the heart* [mind] *of men, proceed evil thoughts, adulteries, fornications, murders, Thefts, covetousness, wickedness, deceit, lasciviousness, an evil eye, blasphemy, pride, foolishness: All these evil things come from within, and defile the man.* In Proverbs (23:7), we read, *For as he* [the "hidden man of the heart," as St. Peter states it in his First Epistle] *thinketh in his heart, so is he.* Therefore when man thinks lack and limitation, want and woe, he brings these evils upon himself in proportion to their occupancy of his thoughts. Just as wrong thinking leads into error, so correct thinking leads man out of all forms of evil and into the abundance of good.

Logically we have a right to conclude that it is the thought that man entertains and fosters in his own mind that is the determining factor for good or evil. Circumstances, environments, education, examples set by others, etc., often lend power and influence, yea, strength to evil suggestions which come to man, but only to the extent that one accepts evil as real, intelligent, and powerful.

For when one sees evil for what it really is—nothing but a false belief,—its seeming reality, influence, intelligence, power, or substance falls by its own weight because evil never has had, has not now, and never can have any reality in any form whatsoever, inasmuch as God is All.

⌈The deciding factor, however, in any given case, is the thought and feeling which a man consciously or unconsciously admits, holds, or cherishes as real and actual in the sacred sanctuary of his own mind.⌉ It is here and here only where a thing (anything) is accepted or rejected, held to or realized; here alone that the seed of any thought or suggestion is planted, germinates, unfolds, and becomes a deciding factor in his life, character, activity, yea, the destiny of his career, the realization of good or evil, abundance or lack and limitation. Really it is in the mind or consciousness of man that his success or failure is determined and put into action and not in his environment, be it good or evil. True, these things may have their influence with man, but only in proportion as man allows these ideas to enter and dominate his mind and action.

Therefore, if a man allows evil lack, limitation, want and woe to enter and dominate his thinking, he will, of necessity, reap as he sows. If he sows evil or limiting thoughts he will surely reap a harvest of sin, lack, limitation, disease and death. On the other hand, if he admits and allows the Christ-idea in man to unfold, take possession of, rule and govern his thinking, as did Jesus, our Exemplar, he will naturally, logically, and invariably bring forth and demonstrate the abundance of good and good only. This in turn will automatically eliminate from his mind, life, character, and experience any and every thing opposed to and unlike God, be it that of sin, disease, fear, lack, limitation, want or woe. Furthermore, he will have a harvest—scant or abundant, good or evil—commensurate with his thinking.

Hence the importance in all our thinking is to banish from our consciousness the belief that substance and supply are in or of matter, and know and realize that it is always spiritual and eternal. Moreover, I find, we must embrace the truth, namely, that it is in divine consciousness, a present reality—now; for God, eternal good, is omnipresent. And as man cannot be separated from his God, Spirit, even so he can never be separated from his true substance and supply.

In order to gain this knowledge of substance one must do as St. Paul did, "die daily" to this world's idea of substance, and be thoroughly alive to the correct, spiritual, God-given idea of it. Then man will live above the false idea of substance, and enjoy freedom of thought and deed, which only the true understanding of it can bring. He will then find that the false idea of substance can not mesmerize him nor enslave him, for he has now come into "the knowing" which Christ said would make man free.

Stand fast therefore in the liberty wherewith Christ hath made us free, and be not entangled again with the yoke of bondage, says Paul; and, *having done all, to stand;* that is, forevermore refuse to believe in or lean upon matter and material money as substance and supply. No other attitude is possible or permissible. Man will also learn that he cannot truly live and enjoy life as God intended him to do, until he gains this true and correct view of substance, and ceases to believe in and depend upon what mortals call substance,—matter. When man comes into this understanding of substance and abides by it, he will manifest it just as freely as he does life.

This understanding must also be gained by the one who has not as yet been called upon to face and demonstrate substance and supply according to the Principle underlying true substance and supply; for its lesson is for all, and covers all good and right ideas of every name and nature.

In Christian Science one does not demonstrate matter substance, for there is no such thing. As man gains the true understanding of the nature of substance, and how to demonstrate it, God finds the way in which it is to be manifested to each and every one of His children who faithfully abide by the Principle of all true being.

When we learn to handle this false belief of substance through Christian Science, we shall find it much easier to handle all human problems, because true substance underlies all things; for God—substance—is All-in-all; the basis or foundation of all; yea, is ALL.

One needs to be alert, however, and carry out Christ's command, *What I say unto you, I say unto all, Watch,* lest one become mesmerized in some way with a false idea of substance, and be led into the belief that there is life, substance, pleasure, and pain in matter, thereby opening his mental door for sin, disease and death to enter.

The Bible and Christian Science teach us that everything proceeds from God consequently all that really is, is the manifestation of this infinite, all-inclusive Mind. Logically, therefore it follows that one must see health and strength mentally in order to have them become manifested: likewise one must learn to see substance mentally in order to have it become manifested. Real health, strength, and substance are spiritual, never in nor of matter, and a present reality.

The Christian Science idea of substance is totally different from the human or mortal mind concept of it. If one is studying Christian Science but has not yet gained the correct view of substance, he, no doubt, will find himself still on the old plane of thought about this all-important subject, and more or less in bondage to lack and limitation, the same as before he came into Christian Science.

It is absolutely imperative that we gain the true and correct understanding of substance and supply, if we wish to avail ourselves of our full birthright. It is likewise just as imperative for man to realize that all good is in the divine Mind, and that it is his duty, right, and privilege to reflect everything that is in the divine Mind. It can only be done, however, proportionately to his correct understanding of God, and man's at-one-ment with his heavenly Father, a loving obedience to Principle, and the unconditional surrender of his human will, desire, aim, purpose, and motive to God. This is seeking the kingdom of God first of all, the outcome of which will in turn show him that all true substance is in and of God; that is, that God is the only true substance there is, hence substance is eternal, unchangeable, omnipresent, and infinite as the eternal I AM.

When this true and correct view of God is gained and man realizes that he has all good because he has God, he then understands that his good is eternal, ever-present, unchangeable, and indestructible as God Himself. Consequently he will not fear what error may try to do; for he now understands that evil is not power, because God is omnipotent—the only power there is. It is, therefore, absolutely imperative that this error—that matter and material money are substance—which has so long gripped mankind, be met and mastered correctly.

To gain this understanding, however, may require more of man than some are at present ready to pay, though all will have to come to it ere they will be able *to see the King in his glory*. The trouble with many is, they would love to have and enjoy these unbounded blessings, but are unwilling to pay the price. An example of such a situation is found in the rich young man, as recorded in the nineteenth chapter of Matthew, who sought of the Master the mode or procedure for him to obey that he might inherit eternal life. Jesus knew instantly the young man's consciousness was darkened by the belief in his material possessions and wealth as being his substance, safety, and supply; a blindness to the reality of substance so great that it demanded the disposal of his material possessions before the understanding of who and what was real substance and supply could be gained. Had the young man recognized God as his true substance and supply, he would never have been called upon to give up his material possessions; but the lesson he needed required it. Likewise it is requisite of every one who is in the same mental darkness.

Another parallel instance was that of Job, who had to suffer the loss of his vast possessions before he could or did awaken to the unreality of matter as substance. Job, however, was more righteous than the rich young man, in that he finally turned to God and was abundantly rewarded: . . . *the Lord gave Job twice as much as he had before* (Job 42:10).

It is so much easier to desire a given success than it is to work for it and gain it step by step, as all must do if we have not already done so. One must be willing to *lay aside every weight,* as Paul says, in order to run his race successfully, and gain the goal.

Jesus said, *If thou wilt be perfect, go and sell that thou hast* [of false and erroneous ideas and beliefs concerning matter and material money as substance], . . . *and come and follow me* [look to God,—Mind alone as your substance and supply]. The price, in short, is to obey and leave all for Christ, Truth. But this does not mean as some religious teachers have taught that one is called upon to give up that which is good: no only error—evil.

Mr. Kimball, my teacher in the Metaphysical College, in Boston, Massachusetts, told me one day, that when he first became actively engaged in the Christian Science work he was so enthusiastic when he saw what could be accomplished through a clear understanding and faithful appliance of its Principle, that he wrote to Mrs. Eddy how deeply grateful he was for Christian Science, and added, that he was willing to give up everything for Science. Mrs. Eddy did not stop to write a letter and send her message by mail, but she wired him and said, "Dear Student: You do not have to give up anything except error."

What we need to give up is our false belief of life, health, strength, pleasure, pain, and substance in matter. It means to come out and *be ye separate,* and give up looking upon, holding to, and leaning upon matter as a reality—as substance.

According to the Scriptures the very first temptation to commit evil that came to man, was the suggestion to look upon and partake of matter as his substance, pleasure, and supply, thus being unwittingly led to forsake the one and only God, and break the First Commandment, *Thou shalt have no other gods before me.* This suggestion, in turn, became the basis or source of all subsequent evil.

When evil had thus mesmerized man into taking this first step in his downward course, it was not long before he began to be suspicious, envious, jealous, selfish, hateful, licentious, murderous, etc. In fact, we find that *every imagination of his heart was only evil continually.*

This being the first transgression, it must be clear to every right-thinking man that the first duty of man, as the Bible teaches us, is to turn from matter and all material things as his substance, pleasure, and supply, retrace his steps to a point where he left the straight and narrow way, and again gain the understanding and realization that Spirit alone is his substance and supply, for there is none other. Here stand until it is made manifest. *For we are made partakers of Christ* [Truth], *if we hold the beginning of our confidence stedfast unto the end* (Hebrews 3:14). When this is realized we must walk faithfully on this highway of holiness, never again looking backward to matter or material things as our substance and supply. Then our reward will be sure and ever-appearing. For *the silver is mine, and the gold is mine, saith the Lord of hosts* (Haggai 2:8). *Fear not, . . . I* [God] *am thy shield, and thy exceeding great reward* (Genesis 15:1).

Let me here emphasize that realization is as important as understanding, for it is understanding made or become operative, and is positively indispensable to the fruition of understanding. Understanding is of little value without a realization thereof. It (understanding without realization) is as the salt that has lost its savour, spoken of by Jesus in the Sermon on the Mount. Realization of the truth of one's understanding in his own consciousness is *the Lord working with them, and confirming the word with signs* [symbols] *following,* spoken of in Mark (16:20), and further confirmed by Jesus in his statement: *. . . ye shall know the truth, and the truth shall make you free* (John 8:32).

There is another class of seekers after this truth, and to these I desire to speak a word of encouragement. They are most earnest and sincere, and perfectly willing and glad to make any and all necessary sacrifice in order to gain this goal of demon-

strating substance and supply on a purely metaphysical basis, but have allowed themselves to be
mesmerized by the false suggestions of evil that
this subject is too deep for them, and the goal too
high for any one in such humble circumstances, or
of such limited education and spiritual attainment
to reach these heights.

But let such a one understand and realize that
this is but a false and evil suggestion which one
needs to guard against most carefully, exclude from
his thoughts, and know that no honest and earnest
seeker after God need despair or become discour-
aged, because God never requires a single step to
be taken by man, except it is fully and easily within the reach of every one of His children who has
glimpsed his at-one-ment with God, and is willing
to learn the lesson of surrendering wholly and unconditionally to God. There is no respecter of persons with God.

You will find your dear heavenly Father always
at your side, tenderly showing you the way, helping you over the seemingly hard, rough, and apparently insurmountable obstacles, and saying, *Be
strong and of a good courage, fear not, nor be
afraid . . . : for the Lord thy God, he it is that doth
go with thee; he will not fail thee, nor forsake thee*
(Deut. 31:6). And again: *Fear not: for I have redeemed thee, I have called thee by thy name; thou*

art mine. When thou passeth through the waters, I will be with thee; and through the rivers, they shall not overflow thee: when thou walkest through the fire, thou shalt not be burned; neither shall the flame kindle upon thee (Isaiah 43:1, 2).

This is amply set forth and demonstrated in the innumerable examples in sacred history. Take, for instance, Abraham, born and reared in the midst of idolatry and worldliness, who boldly but lovingly stepped forth and faithfully followed the gentle leadings of Truth and Love, finally finding himself in the Land of Promise—"the land of milk and honey," and revealed of God as the father of the faithful.

Moses is another instance of how God called him when he was but an humble sheepherder, as was also the case of David, "the sweet singer of Israel." The dauntless Daniel and the three worthies were young captives among a strange and foreign people; all are worthy examples.

The apostles were nearly all fishermen or men in meager circumstances and St. Paul was a tent-maker when God called them to a higher activity based upon a clearer understanding of Himself as revealed unto them. Today they stand forth as mountain peaks and beacon lights to all mankind, proving, beyond any doubt, what man can do through this higher, fuller, more comprehensive and correct understanding, and an absolute loving obedience to and an unreserved and radical reliance on the Principle of all true being, God.

What one must do is to go and do likewise; follow as God opens the way and abundantly enables man to make the demonstration that God is his substance and supply of all good this present moment; also that this door of opportunity has never been, is not now, and never can be closed to him by man or devil—evil.

That man may be able and in a proper mental and spiritual condition to receive, appreciate, and make proper use of the abundance of all good, as provided by his heavenly Father, omnipotent Mind, it is absolutely imperative that one must be thoroughly prepared to receive and make fit usage of this unlimited, God-bestowed heritage.

Do not men always have to pay for what they receive? If one tumbles into a soft berth now and then, without working or paying for it, does he not usually fall down sooner or later? Man must be ready for God's blessings in order to receive them. Otherwise, the sudden possession of affluence might prove a curse to man instead of a blessing, as in the case of the "Prodigal Son," who, so far as the record of him is given, may have been, and no doubt was a normal and average young man, until he came into the sudden possession of wealth and worldly goods. Because of his lack of spiritual preparedness, he sadly failed to understand, appreciate, and make proper use of it. One can never really and truly enter this promised land of all good by any other way. It must be according to God's requirements. *Verily, verily, I say unto you, He that entereth not by the door into the sheepfold, but climbeth up some other way, the same is a thief and a robber* (John 10:1).

I know of nothing that demands such a high, clear, and wholly unselfish mental and spiritual state as does the demonstration of proving that God is the only and true substance and supply of man. To me it is plain that it is getting back in spirit and deed to have but one God, and keep the First Commandment in spirit and in Truth. It must become apparent to every careful thinker who believes in the Bible that the moment he looks upon, holds to, and depends upon aught but God for his substance and supply, he is breaking the First Commandment, *Thou shalt have no other gods before me.*

In order to enter this holy and sacred place of the Most High, one must unloose the sandals of his own self-righteousness and be thoroughly willing to be shown his shortcomings, to have his turbid mentality stirred and purified; yea, he must be willing to have the tares of human will, selfishness, self-will, self-seeking, self-justification, self-indulgence, hate, and malice cleared out, roots and all; and to be purged of greed, lust, love of money, etc. This mental purgation and preparedness must be worked out in the consciousness of the rich and poor alike, inasmuch as there is no respect of persons with God. *The voice of him that crieth in the wilderness, Prepare ye the way of the Lord, make straight in the desert a highway for our God. Every valley shall be exalted, and every mountain and hill shall be made low: and the crooked shall be made straight, and the rough places plain: And the glory of the Lord shall be revealed, and all flesh shall see it together· for the mouth of the Lord hath spoken it* (Isaiah 40:3-5).

One will find that *It is easier for a camel to go through the eye of a needle* than for one to truly make the demonstration if he is not mentally and spiritually prepared to enter this sacred domain and enjoy and make proper use of the fulness of Gods' promises. Even after the disciples had been under the personal tutorship of the Master for three years, he found that they were not even then prepared to receive and make use of the many things he had to tell them. When he was about to depart to his Father and our Father, he commanded them to go to Jerusalem and tarry there until they should receive the Holy Spirit. But, in examining the records, we find that this promise was not fulfilled until the disciples had been emptied of error, so far as they saw and understood it, and had come into one accord with God's requirements and with each other. When thus prepared to receive this higher blessing and larger legacy, it flowed into their consciousness as naturally as the sun dissipates the darkness. Mrs. Eddy, in all her writings, is most insistent that the soil of the heart be made ready; and she strongly emphasizes the fact that it is the real Christian who most readily fathoms Christian Science.

The great fact is, one must be strictly honest in his endeavor to seek this fulness of substance and supply; that is, he must not seek this blessing in order to gratify his senses, or live extravagantly; nor must he seek it because of his love for money; but he must seek it purely because it is God's will to man that he should be able to demonstrate and enjoy the fulness of all good, the abundance of substance and supply of every name and nature needful.

The attainment of this correct understanding of substance and its application to our daily needs, I find, includes vastly more than appears on the surface. It includes among other things, a higher, fuller, more comprehensive and correct understand-

ing of the divine Principle—God, and of man's at-
one-ment with his heavenly Father; absolute reliance on and a loving obedience to God, with an
unconditional surrender of our human will to Him;
also to seek, know, and do His will in everything
so far as we understand it today. Jesus Christ said:
*I seek not mine own will, but the will of the Father
which hath sent me* (John 5:30). Furthermore, the
thought must be spiritualized, and when these
points are won, matter will be seen to be nothing
more than a false belief,—never real substance and
supply.

In the amplitude of my religious experience I
have come to the conscientious conclusion that
there is nothing in all our service to God calling for
more watchfulness, or for a more conscientious and
unswerving holding of the needle of our spiritual
compass so steadfastly and unceasingly pointing to
God, and God only, than does the demonstration
of the fact that God is man's only substance and
supply—his ALL-in-all.

If one allows himself to be influenced or
swayed, even in a degree, to look to or depend
upon mortal man, mortal mind ideas or promises,
or matter as substance and supply, he will miss
his course and be obliged to retrace his footsteps.

The reason for this unceasing vigilance cannot
be emphasized too strongly, because man is now

turning away absolutely from looking to, or leaning upon aught but God; that is, he is now, to the best of his understanding and ability, literally keeping the First Commandment and having no other gods but the God of Israel.

One who has thus surrendered wholly to God, seeks only God's guidance in thought and deed, and is willing and glad to await God, as did Daniel when he was in the lions' den. Not only that, but he is content to abstain from murmuring and pitying himself, not only audibly, but in the innermost chambers of his heart; and he looks away from every form of matter and mortal man to God. Having gained this much he is willing to take all necessary human footsteps, doing whatsoever his hand findeth to do, and doing it as unto God. He stops outlining ways and means, and lets God find the channel or channels through which substance may flow into his life. He is also grateful for this purifying process, even if it be "as by fire"; for he now realizes it will rejuvenate and prepare him—a vital necessity, as we have already seen—to receive and make proper use of the blessings he is seeking, and which God has prepared for them who love and obey Him. It will also bring him a clearer understanding and realization of his sonship, as well as of his oneness with the Father; a knowledge and realization that there is no other substance than

God; and that the supply of all his needs is found in the infinity of ever-present good.

I shall never forget when I began to understand and realize that God's promises were simply God's eternal laws. Then some of the deep things of God unfolded to me anew, and I saw that God had decreed from eternity the great fact that He had provided the abundance of all good for each and every one of His children who were willing to seek and gain the true understanding, and lovingly obey His precepts.

I also found that God's promises to Abraham, Isaac, and Jacob, as well as to the children of Israel, were simply God's eternal, unchangeable, and ever operative laws. In Isaiah 41:10 we read: *Fear thou not; for I am with thee;* meaning that God has bound Himself—through his eternal law—to be with man, be his God, his strength, his helper, and his upholder.

God's promise that *There shall no evil befall thee, neither shall any plague come nigh thy dwelling* (Psalms 91:10), is simply another of His laws. So is the promise that *no good thing will he withhold from them that walk uprightly* (Psalms 84:11); and *Come unto me, all ye that labour and are heavy laden, and I will give you rest* (Matt. 11:28). These and all of God's promises are really nothing less than God's eternal and unchangeable laws through which He has voluntarily pledged and bound Himself to give to man all good. These promises—laws—are as sure and as truly demonstrable as are the problems in mathematics, when one understands them and obeys them one hundred per cent.

In the world of material accomplishment mankind views the wondrous strides made visible in such lines of endeavor as instanced in communication—from human messengers afoot to the telephone, telegraph, and radio; again, in transportation—from ox, ass, and horse to the railroad, the automobile, and the aeroplane; but when we carefully consider the religious development by searching and scrutinizing the writings of the early church Fathers, and the religious writings and sermons from thence on and up to the time Mrs. Eddy appeared upon the religious horizon and gave to the world the Christ Science, we are forced to acknowledge that little advancement had been accomplished. One reason for this is the fact that mankind has failed to grasp the full and complete salvation provided by God for the deliverance of mankind, not only from sin as generally accepted, but from the thraldom of disease, lack, limitation, want and woe as well.

The cause of this lack of real and progressive development along spiritual lines has no doubt been largely due to the lamentable fact that error has misled both saint and sinner to have an entirely wrong view and understanding of God's mercy.

When we analyze the average man's conception of God's mercy, we shall find that it really amounts to a license to do wrong, in a limited sense at least; for he figures if he falls down or yields to temptation now and then, because he thinks of himself as a poor miserable mortal, and cannot be expected to be one hundred per cent perfect in the flesh, he presumes that God, in His mercy, will forgive him his shortcomings. True, God will forgive him, but he will also find that he will never enter into the full understanding and realization of his sonship, and all that this includes, until he stops all wrong doing. In other words, should he continue this zig-zag method of sinning and repenting, he will, ere long, discover that his progress will be exceedingly slow; and he will, furthermore, become aware of his inability to demonstrate his birthright. Neither will he get his answer, *Well done, good and faithful servant,* any more than he will get his answer to a problem in mathematics if he deviates but once from the principle underlying his problem; for God, who is unchangeable—the same yesterday, today, and forever—requires absolute obedience to all His laws and dependence upon Him as the Principle of all true being. There is no hypocrisy in serving God. Paul states it thus: *Be not deceived; God is not mocked: for whatsoever a man soweth, that shall he also reap* (Gal. 6:7).

It is true that man cannot find his perfection in matter, or in the mortal, human concept of man. He must therefore, demonstrate over and out of matter into the consciousness and realization of his true, real, and spiritual selfhood, because he, the real man, has always been, is now, and ever will be, God's child—the perfect image and likeness of God.

St. John states it thus: *Whosoever abideth in him sinneth not: Whosoever sinneth hath not seen him, neither knoweth him. . . . He that committeth sin is of the devil; for the devil sinneth from the beginning. For this purpose the Son of God was manifested, that he might destroy the works of the devil. Whosoever is born of God doth not commit sin; for his seed remaineth in him: and he* [the true spiritual man] *cannot sin, because he is born of God.*

St. Paul, in his epistle to the Romans, warns us against this false and misleading belief concerning God's mercy in these unmistakable words: *What shall we say then? Shall we continue in sin, that grace may abound? God forbid. How shall we, that are dead to sin, live any longer therein? . . . Know ye not, that to whom ye yield yourselves servants to obey, his servants ye are to whom ye*

*obey; whether of sin unto death, or of obedience
unto righteousness?* And St. John adds, . . . *and
there shall in no wise enter into it* [the heavenly
Jerusalem—harmonious existence] *anything that
defileth, . . . or maketh a lie.*

Again, one may be given to exclaim, . . . *God so
loved the world, that he gave his only begotten
Son, that whosoever believeth in him should not
perish, but have everlasting life* (John 3:16). True,
but man seems to forget the fact that Jesus had to
be one hundred per cent obedient; and he is our
Exemplar; so where is there any way of escape
from keeping the command of having one God,
one substance, and one supply?

The First and great Commandment must be
correctly understood and obeyed, now or hereafter,
by every man, woman, and child before the complete heavenly harmony can be obtained and enjoyed, together with the realization of all good, no
matter how much or how little of this world's good
one seems to possess, or that he believes he has
acquired by his own intelligence and effort. All
must learn sooner or later that if he makes any
thought, idea or so-called material substance substance, aside from God, he is leaning upon and
adhering to something besides God, and consequently is having another god, thereby breaking

the First and greatest of all Commandments, *Thou shalt have no other gods before me.*

God requires absolute obedience. Even Moses failed to enter the Promised Land, although he repeatedly pleaded with God to forgive him for his disobedience at Meribah-Kadesh and let him enter. And why? Simply because, in the midst of the clamouring of the Children of Israel for water, he struck the rock in place of just speaking to it as God had commanded him. God demanded of Moses absolute obedience. Is it reasonable then to expect that God, who is no respecter of persons, will be less exacting with mankind of today, who has all the God-given and untold advantages in the form of revelations, examples, and religious enlightenment, than He was with His self-denying and faithful servant Moses?

Again, one must not try to help himself out of financial difficulties by borrowing; for this, I have found, increases his troubles. Neither must he seek substance and supply for material gain, nor in order to spend it upon lustful pursuits, self-indulgence, or for the sake of hoarding it. Man seeks the substance and supply of the abundance of good because it is his birthright as a child of God, created to express or reflect and to enjoy the presence, power, fulness, and harmony of God—a demonstration of the perpetual abundance of all good, not only for his own harmonious existence but to fulfill his share of responsibility in assisting or helping mankind with it.

The Science of Mind, and all that pertains to it, needs to be understood and strictly adhered to in order that one may demonstrate all his problems on a truly scientific basis. I find, however, that most people do not do this, and consequently they endeavor to demonstrate, as for instance, substance and supply on a purely material plane. But as one comes into the sacred understanding and realization of what true substance is, and how to demonstrate it according to the Principle of Christian Science, he must take another forward step and stop outlining, or in any way depending upon or figuring his ability or inability to meet his numerous obligations by counting on anything material or mortal whatsoever, be it that of his weekly paycheck, salary, position, employer, business, dividends, commissions, bonuses, or on a man's promise to aid him or to do for him. Neither must he count on any deal or sale, whether it be real estate or merchandise of any name or nature, as his substance and supply: no, not even if a business transaction has proceeded far enough to be in escrow, and money has been paid down to bind the bargain. Neither must he look to or count upon money due him from any good and legitimate business transaction, be it ever so gilt-edged, as his substance and supply. Neither must he look upon any earthly possession, or money in hand or in the bank as his substance and supply. Not only this, but he must be careful and not look even to the seeming human channel or channels through which material substance may flow to him, or through which it has been flowing into his life before he undertook to demonstrate substance and supply on a purely scientific basis.

To be exact, one must cease to look to, believe in, count upon, hold to, or lean upon anything material or human whatsoever as his substance and supply. One must learn to look to God and God only—the All-in-all—as his substance and supply. This cannot be stated too often, nor emphasized too strongly. In Isaiah we read (Chap. 42:8): *I am the Lord: that is my name: and my glory will I not give to another, neither my praise to graven images.*

One of the most subtle of error's suggestions relative to business transactions, be they great or small, I have noted in my long experience, is that wherein one may have a deal pending and even practically consummated, with a date agreed upon for the payment, at which time one is to receive the earnings or settlement accruing to him. In this instance the great danger, while waiting for the pay-

ment, lies in accepting the many plausible suggestions which are sure to come to one at this particular time, among which are, namely, to purchase
something wanted, and satisfying one's actions with
the thought that he can and will pay the amount
upon the receipt of his believed-in earned emolu-
ment. Another, equally as subtle, is the suggestion
to plan how he can and will disburse the money
believed to be justly accruing to him in liquidating,
say, his obligations, and in purchasing something
needed or desired.

Such mental activity on the part of one is positively erroneous, absolutely inadmissible, and dangerous to the successful culmination of the transaction, inasmuuch as it causes one to deviate from
the straight course of looking steadfastly to God
as his only substance and supply, and for the time
being, looking to and counting upon matter as his
substance and supply.

I find one must learn to keep his mental door
guarded and closed to any and every suggestion of
counting upon aught but God to meet one's every
human need, and lovingly and confidently wait on
God to consummate the deal successfully. He
never fails. He will bring it to pass if it is a just
and right activity; but you must trust Him implicitly, which means, in our modern way of express-

ing it, to keep our hands off, that is never try to steady the Ark (2 Sam. 6:6, 7), leaving God to bring out the result. *Wait on the Lord, and keep his way, and he shall exalt thee to inherit the land* (Psalms 37:34).

Too great stress cannot be placed upon one of the pitfalls error cunningly produces at this point; and this evil, I feel, should be uncovered to the earnest seeker. This error deals with a situation wherein one is almost wholly unconscious of its subtilty, and is a least thought-of brand of trickery. We will review it thus. When one has worked to know his supply is ever-present and available, and sees it demonstrated, say, through a sale, the error immediately begins to lead one's thought away from God, by causing him to feel and reason that now he has substance and supply in his possession; thus losing sight of the fact that he has always had, has now, and always will have the ever-available supply, providing he understands why this is so through the realization of his at-one-ment as the reflecting image of God, Mind; living in obedience to Principle, God, and deviating not one iota from a constant and loving holding to God as his only source of substance and supply. When it comes, he must be watchful lest he forget God. God warned the Children of Israel as they were entering Canaan, not to forget Him in their prosperity.

At other times one's consciousness may be darkened by a desire to seek further manifestations of supply for the benefit of himself only, not considering that his existence is in reality bound up in a like service of expressing good to his brother, the expression of service that makes true the words of Jesus when he admonished his disciples that he *came not to be ministered* [served] *unto, but to minister* [serve] (Matt. 20:28), showing that the highest form of service is the purely unselfish one, or the seeking of your own good in the welfare of another of God's ideas—your fellow-man.

To seek and see the fulfilment of such action or service, with its attendant blessings for all, one must look to God to direct his pathway to the individual or group to whom the service that is for him to express or manifest, would be a blessing. But to try to dispose of anything to your fellow-man with one's own consciousness filled with a sense of gaining his own supply as a greater necessity than that of producing good for his brother, is not love, but is a type of selfishness, fear, and the practice of dishonesty. We are all salesmen, to a large degree, in that we are disposing of service of some type or sort; and those who seem to be engaged in physical efforts alone, are selling or disposing of some part of the whole of an idea—even the man who is digging a sewer-ditch—that enhances the happiness and protection of his fellow-man.

One does not always mean to look away from God; but the belief in material money as man's substance and supply is constantly suggesting itself in so many ways or avenues that he must stand guard over his mental acceptances.

Another great blessing to me has been the understanding and realization that all responsibility for the successful manifestation and its resultant harmony rests upon God's shoulders. *Commit thy way unto the Lord; trust also in him; and he shall bring it to pass,* advised the Psalmist. One must get rid of the sense of personal responsibility; for if one is God's image or reflection, as the Bible affirms, wherein can he be or is he endowed with a sense of personal responsibility? God alone is responsible for the success, the increase, or the victory. The government is upon His shoulders.

When Moses was obedient and left the responsibility on God's shoulders where it belonged, he never failed to do and to accomplish what God commanded him to do, whether before Pharaoh or the Red Sea. Neither did Joshua fail. He was told to have the priests take the Ark of the Covenant, march out and stand in the middle of Jordan, and that the river, which at this particular time was overflowing its banks, would cease its flow the instant the soles of the feet of the priests would touch the water. This servant of God realized that it was not his responsibility, nor the responsibility of his people. It was, though, his responsibility to obey God implicitly. When he did this, God took care of the rest.

Again, note the lack of any responsibility being assumed by the three worthies, Daniel's associates in capitivity, who also placed the responsibility for their protection on God. Their only responsibility was to respond to God's ability to protect them.

When the disciples worried over the feeding of the thousands of people who came out into the desert to listen to the Master, Christ taught them, and all mankind, too, this same lesson, namely, that all they were called upon to do, was to leave the whole responsibility with God, obey Christ's commands to seat the people, and serve the broken bread and fish to the multitude, the abundance of which produced twelve full baskets over and above their needs. This excess of requirement not only illustrated the abundance of supply to man, but in addition denoted the mental harmony provided through a realization of the superabundance of good.

Such illustrations show God's protecting care, government, and supply; that He alone is responsible for the manifestation and fulfilment of His own promise to those who rely on Him; and thus demonstrating to man the unfailing law of the infinite I AM.

All that man has to do is to lose his sense of personal responsibility in the matter, and understand, realize, and put into active practice his own small part of lovingly obeying God, and unreservedly rely upon God's ability and willingness to provide all good needful to man. To explain more clearly: the responsibility of man is his willingness to abdicate his belief in his own importance and responsibility, thus permitting God to express His inexhaustible supply of all good necessary. *Commit thy way unto the Lord; trust also in him, and he shall bring it to pass* (Psalms 37:5).

Another insidious error which almost always tries to tempt man, even before and after a business transaction is being or has been consummated, is that of telling of it to others—one's asociates, friends, or even the immediate family.

The wise and prudent course to pursue is the one practiced by Nehemiah when he went up, at God's command, to Jerusalem to repair the broken-down wall of that city. He told no man what God had put in his heart to do—not even the Jews, the rulers, or the priests, keeping his own counsel and thus completing his work unmolested by friend or foe.

Christ himself laid down the rule when he said unto the blind man whom he healed, *See that no man know it.* Again, in his parable of the man who discovered the "pearl of great price," and who strictly kept his own counsel. Note how this man went and hid it in the chambers of his own mind, and in doing so, he found no difficulty in consummating the deal.

It is absolutely imperative to be obedient to the Master's injunction. Otherwise you invite interference, delay, hindrance, and ofttimes your own defeat by permitting tares to be sown in your field.

It is, furthermore, inadmissible and folly to expose ourselves to minds many, and invite our own downfall, as did Peter when he boasted of his unswerving loyalty to Jesus on the eve of his Master's crucifixion. *A fool uttereth all his mind; but a wise man keepeth it in till afterwards* (Proverbs 29:11).

Mortal mind, or one who accepts matter or material money as substance and supply, may cry out, *Who then can be saved?* as did the disciples and the people who listened to Jesus when he so clearly and emphatically warned them—in the tenth chapter of Mark—against this false and misleading sense, namely, that matter is substance. Jesus answered and pointed out to them in this appeal for understanding, that *With men this is impossible, but not with God: for with God all things are possible;* thus placing this understanding and realization within the reach of every man, woman, and child—God being their helper and sure reward, and assuming all responsibility.

One does not murmur when working out a problem in addition, say, because he must adhere absolutely and unconditionally to the principle of mathematics. He knows he has no alternative. Then why should he lament over the strict demands of the Principle of all true being which applies to substance and supply, remembering that Jesus said, *No man can serve two masters: . . . Ye cannot serve God and mammon* (Matt. 6:24): and again: . . . *strait is the gate, and narrow is the way, which leadeth unto life, and few there be that find it* (Matt 7:14).

One must, of course, be grateful to God for any and every evidence of good which supplies his human needs; but he must be ever awake to the great fact that God, and God alone, is his only real substance and supply. God's promise or eternal law is, . . . *those that seek me early shall find me . . . I lead in the way of righteousness, in the midst of the paths of judgment: That I may cause those that love me to inherit substance; and I will fill their treasures* (Proverbs, Chap. 8).

One should also realize that he must be ever faithful, doing everything his hand findeth to do; or as Paul admonishes, . . . *whatsoever ye do, do it heartily, as to the Lord, and not unto men; Knowing that of the Lord ye shall receive the reward of the inheritance: for ye serve the Lord Christ* (Col. 3:23-24). At the same time one must realize that it is not through his own ability and human effort that he achieves success, but that it is *God that giveth the increase* (1 Cor. 3:7), and *hath gotten him the victory* (Psalms 98:1). In other words he must hold steadfastly and as conscientiously to the Principle underlying all true substance and supply as he holds to the principle underlying his problem in mathematics. If he does this lovingly and faithfully, his answer in the form of substance and supply will invariably be his without fail; for it is God's law that no good thing will be withheld from them that love and obey Him. And he will eventually hear, too, Christ's commendation in these words, *Well done, thou good and faithful servant: thou hast been faithful over a few things, I will make thee ruler over many things: enter thou into the joy of thy lord* (Matt. 25:21).

My many years of endeavor in the practice of Christian Science, together with a constant study of the Bible and of *Science and Health With Key*

to The Scriptures, has made clear to me the understanding one must have and keep in consciousness,
when destroying the seeming effects of falsities and
their claims of manifestation. Because of divergent
situations or conditions the mental work required, I
find, takes on opposite ministrations. To illustrate:
when disease is the belief, you unsee disease—that
it is no part of the ever-living God, Life, which you
but reflect; that is, you reflect or manifest only
what God, Mind, knows is true, eternal, and harmonious. Thus you destroy and wipe it out of consciousness. When eliminated from consciousness
by such mental activity it automatically disappears.

Digressing for the moment from the illustration,
yet bringing the reader's power of reasoning into
alignment with and apropos to the illustration, is it
not a natural thing to discern that God, being eter-
nally all-harmonious and continually expressing
Himself in man, made by Him in His (God's) own
likeness to express the very essence of His being,
could at no time and in no degree create a sick,
sinning, inharmonious image of Himself?

It is, therefore, by such enlightening thoughts
flooding one's consciousness, and held to continu-
ously as the truth of man's perfection (as image),
that the errors of belief accepted for the moment
as having entity—as real,—in opposition to reality,

no matter how forceful and severe seem the suggestions, are destroyed.

Returning to the second part of the illustration, that of the mental activity in working out the truth concerning harmony, position, or substance and supply, let us note the divergent method of overcoming the seeming inharmony.

In this instance, one must see and realize harmony, position, and substance and supply as a present reality—not going to be because of any effort or labor you put forth to make it a fact:—and, furthermore, you dwell right in the midst of it. Moreover, you live and move and have your being, as St. Paul advises (Acts 17:28), in God, infinite Mind, where all good has been, is now, and ever will be— an absolute and undeniable fact.

Is it not more natural, and divinely so, when one considers it thoughtfully,—weighs it truthfully with the Scriptural enlightenment of the creation of God's creating, which, in truth, is the expression of God's being,—to see and realize that as image and likeness of the only presence there is, namely, God, that you, without volition, do manifest harmony; that you are in your rightful position—in the activity that God, Mind, so wills His image to perform? Too, wherein then, could fear of lack or limitation, or yet per contra, even a thought or desire for place or power gain a foothold in consciousness? Everything needful to supply one's need,—the position and the power to express harmonious, joyful activity in that position,—is now, and always will be man's birthright as God's son—His image. Likewise the substance and supply of everything needful to man is an idea in Mind, God; and as image, man has it now.

Is it not logical that as man—you and I,—holding tenaciously to our birthright as God's image, do express the infinite supply of the one great cause and substance of all that is—God? And, furthermore, it is not only divinely natural, but it is the law of God that such understanding realized and held to as true in one's own consciousness, must unequivocally produce, here and now, the symbol emblematic of substance in a form, outline, color, and character to meet our state of consciousness, and which can be understood and utilized.

Metaphysically, then, it is the power of the knowing of the truth in Christ's way (John 8:32) that produces upon your consciousness the realization thereof.

Mortal man and material things may seem to have something to do with substance and supply, position or harmony; but one will quickly learn from the Bible and Christian Science of the utter falsity of such beliefs. Mortal man and material things have not one thing to do with or say about man's substance and supply; and this truth will be recognized by man when he understands and realizes his birthright, and his forever designated duty as a child of God, to abundantly reflect and manifest the never-failing supply of the allness of good of every name or nature.

I find that all must come into this understanding and realization that Spirit alone is substance and supply if they have not already obtained this goal,—the rich and poor alike. The man who finds himself chained by the false beliefs of lack and limitation must arise and gain his freedom and God-given birthright—the abundance of all good. The seeming well-to-do brother who has apparently all he needs, and knows no lack or limitation, but who has not come into the possession of his seeming wealth through the correct understanding and realization of true substance and supply, must also gain this true understanding and realization of all good, or he will be classed with the man whom Jesus, in the parable given in the twelfth chapter of Luke, called, "thou fool," when uttering his warning against this false way of reasoning. Or be classed among such as Christ found in the church of the Laodiceans which is described as follows:

Because thou sayest, I am rich, and increased with goods, and have need of nothing; and knowest not that thou are wretched, and miserable, and poor, and blind, and naked: I counsel thee to buy of me gold tried in the fire, that thou mayest be rich; and white raiment, that thou mayest be clothed, and that the shame of thy nakedness do not appear; and anoint thine eyes [discernment] *with eye-salve* [understanding and realization], *that thou mayest see. As many as I love, I rebuke and chasten: be zealous therefore, and repent. Behold, I stand at the door and knock: if any man hear my voice, and open the door, I will come in to him, and will sup with him, and he with me. To him that overcometh will I grant to sit with me in my throne, even as I also overcame, and am set down with my Father in his throne* (Rev. 3:17-21).

I find that one needs to be most careful, deeply conscientious and thoroughly awake mentally as to that upon which he leans and accepts as his substance and supply. In this specific demonstration above all others, error seems to be more subtle and determined in its attempt to deceive by leading one to believe in, hold to and depend, for instance, upon his own effort, upon matter, material money, a person, place, or thing as substance and supply. Often this attempt is found deceiving the very elect.

Should evil or error fail to delude one who is thus honestly holding to and seeking to demonstrate Spirit, God, as his substance and supply, its effects may be found hidden in a more subtle effort to mislead him into believing in and looking upon honorable and legitimate channels of endeavor as the source of his substance and supply instead of the ever-present I AM.

Failing in this, error may further endeavor to befog the seeker by causing him to believe the channel has ceased to exist, such as the loss of his position or property, or a cessation of the purchase of his wares. But the truth is that his channel is just as omnipresent as is his substance and supply. To at once offset this most subtle error, he must realize that God provides both the supply and the channel through which it is manifested, thus taking both the channel and the supply out of the hands of mortals, and placing them where they belong at all times and under every and all circumstances, i.e. in God, thereby teaching man that he is always free and in bondage to no man; for man is owned and governed by God only.

How deeply this error of dependence has seemed to engraft itself, is instanced in a child being led to believe in and look upon his parents as his support, therefore his substance and supply;

or a wife, who considers her husband as the source of her supply. In both instances they are only channels. To these illustrations add the man working for wages or salary, who looks upon his employer as the source of his income or supply; while the employer depends upon his belief in his own sagacity and business acumen to produce supply from the business which he believes he controls.

Even so, every man in his respective line of endeavor, be it that of miner, farmer, manufacturer, laborer, banker, or yet one who has fallen heir to a fortune and believes he needs do no labor other than clip coupons of earned interest, must learn now or later, here or hereafter, that God alone is the one and only source—is his only substance and supply,—and not his own individual effort or endeavor, nor any of the so-called material ideas with which he seems occupied, and of a certainty, no other human being. This will take his idea of substance and supply out of matter, material things, mortal mind or human personalities, and forever place it in God, Spirit, the source of all good, as his only substance and supply, where it belongs.

When he reaches this point he will understand and realize that God is his employer, and the one and only business there is, is God's. Because he now understands and realizes that his work, position, opportunity, business, standing, substance and supply, in fact, everything needful is here, and now—a present reality, for the plain and simple reason that it exists in the eternal, unchangeable, ever-present, divine Mind;—not going to be, but is so now. Consequently he will not be disturbed or moved by the seeming loss of material employment or lack of business for he now realizes that .it is all in God, and he will be able to say with David: *God is our refuge and strength, a very present help in trouble. Therefore will not we fear, though the earth be removed, and though the mountains be carried into the midst of the sea; Though the waters thereof roar and be troubled, though the mountains shake with the swelling thereof . . . There is a river, the streams whereof shall make glad the city of God, the holy place of the tabernacles of the most High. God is in the midst of her; she shall not be moved: God shall help her, and that right early* (Psalms 46:1-5).

It is my earnest desire to so relate of these matters, which have been a part of my own experience and labors in learning to understand the Bible and the teachings of Mrs. Eddy, and applying them successfully, that I trust I am describing them in such a plain, simple, lucid manner that the reader may grasp and begin to realize for himself (if he has not already done so) the way open to him in obtaining God's blessings and the abundance of all good. For it is divinely unnatural that God's image or likeness, His reflected glory and idea, which man is, could in reality suffer lack and limitation, want and woe, when he understands and realizes his true relationship to God.

You do not have to think or worry about your success. Your duty is to understand, realize, and rely unreservedly upon the fact or truth that God IS—not going to be—your abundant success and supply; just as He is your life, health, strength, intelligence, etc. It is God's law that you—His image or likeness (reflection)—manifest God in the form of success and abundance when you lovingly obey His requirements.

Man is often willing, yea, anxious for God or anything that can remove that which mortal, material sense says is painful and harmful to said material sense; but he is not always so willing to let go or part with all forms of evil, especially that which it (material sense) calls good, pleasant, or profitable. Yet everything which proceeds from this so-called mortal mind and sense is evil. Good comes only from the one and only source—God; *For of him, and through him, and to him, are all things* (Romans 11:36). Hence everything which does not proceed from the true source is evil. God recognizes only the good. Therefore, we must learn to distinguish between good and evil of every name and nature. Only good—God's will—brings harmony and peace.

As long as one believes that any material belief, condition, or thing brings harmony, he will be loath to part with it. But all must finally advance and become as willing for God to take away evil and error of every sort as we are for Him to bestow all good.

Remember this, that all evil will eventually result in discord and suffering if its indulgence is not stopped, and the evil removed through Truth and Love. One must stop following his own inclinations and desires, and learn to do God's will.

It is truly wonderful, yea, sublime, how this understanding of, loving obedience to, and reliance on Principle brings out, in turn, one of the most beautiful traits of Christian character, namely, resignation to the will of God.

To be thus wholly and unreservedly resigned to the will of God includes infinitely more than one can comprehend who has not as yet learned the lesson of surrendering his human will to God. How utterly lacking is his realization of the joy, peace, and harmony that fills the heart and consciousness of one who has gained this point in his Christian experience, and can truthfully, humbly, and lovingly look up to God, and say with Jesus, the Christ, *Not my will, but thine, be done.*

Again, how totally ignorant is the man, who has not reached this spiritual unfoldment, of the many seeming severe lessons and experiences often necessary in order to gain this advanced position of a truly Christian life; the innumerable struggles, prayers, supplications, tears, and self-sacrifice known only to the one who has thus come into this great and glorious enlightenment of godliness, and the setting forth of the Christ-spirit which animated the Saviour.

Through many years of close, conscientious study of the Bible, of *Science and Health with Key to the Scriptures,* and the minor writings of Mrs. Eddy, together with the daily practice of the Principle underlying all true being, I have learned that the Biblical basis of demonstrating substance and supply is very simple when once understood, and it is within the reach of every earnest and honest seeker after this glorious goal.

The seeker must be willing, however, to lovingly give himself unto God, freely abandoning his human will, selfishness, self-indulgence, etc., and humbly seek to know and do God's will in all things and at all times in so far as he discerns and understands them from day to day. He must also thoroughly abandon and destroy in his own consciousness—through this glorious understanding of true substance—any belief in, trust in, or any leaning upon matter or material money as his substance and supply.

You may ask, how is one to determine and define between the material method of gaining substance, so-called, and the true spiritual or metaphysical method of demonstrating substance and supply?

My observation of the material method of securing so-called substance and supply is, that it is nothing more or less than the worldly sense of obtaining a given object by laboring for it with that one thought in view. It is not demonstration, but the Adam-sense of acquirement.

I find that scientific demonstration is knowing, first of all, that every good thing is an idea of God, and that the object is cognized not as matter, but as being a type or symbol of true substance. In other words, it is an idea in Mind—the Mind or substance "That makes a thing what it is: its essence" (Webster). This Mind is both the substance and supply of the given idea to its image and likeness,— man.

Material sense would claim the subjective idea, when manifested, to be a material object; but this is not true, the idea taking only the form, outline, color, and character of our belief about it (not its spiritual reality), and thus it meets the human sense of need.

When this is clearly understood and man is living in obedience to God's loving commands, the fear of lack, limitation, and poverty is being erased from consciousness with the realization that the supply of all good is a constant accompaniment of the reflecting image (man) of God. Tomorrow is of no consequence, it exists only in a supposed human mind or consciousness. To God and His idea, man, the only time there is, is the eternal now. Tomorrow is, therefore, just the continuance of reflected spiritual and eternal Life, God, who is substance and supply. Certainly God, Mind, is the power that manifests His infinite supply of spiritual realities and seen in the symbols denoting His presence, or God with us continually. *The blessing of the Lord, it maketh rich, and he addeth no sorrow with it* (Prov. 10:22).

To him on whom this light or understanding is just dawning, and to him who has resolved to at once go forward into proving for himself these explained truths with an honest desire—for desire, if righteous, is but a similitude of prayer—it is imperative that he look to Mind alone for his daily guidance; for human desires and opinions must be obliterated. God lovingly obligates man to this dethronement of human will, and in doing so we have

Christ's command, to *Take therefore no thought for the morrow: for the morrow shall take thought for the things of itself* (Matt. 6:34).

When each new day dawns with its human footsteps to be taken, I find it is well to know and realize anew that God is not only going to be my guidance, but is so here and now. I wait and listen for the *still small voice,* and when the gentle impressions of Spirit appear and become manifest to my consciousness, I follow them, for they invariably lead me to the goal set before me by God, and enable me to perform the task that is for me to execute. *In all thy ways acknowledge him, and he will direct thy paths* (Prov. 3:6).

There may be, perhaps, some suggestions lurking in consciousness that must be cast out—suggestions are often appearing. Self-will, for instance, wherein we find ourselves outlining certain demonstrations which we desire made manifest along lines or channels that we believe will be harmonious—a preconceived belief on our part. Again, wondering or possibly worrying as to whether our efforts of the day will bring, or have in them, certain financial gain.

Under such circumstances and mental condition, I find one needs to turn away from these falsities and temptations of looking to matter and our own human efforts, abandon our own human will, and lovingly and unreservedly turn to and wait on God, and affirm with Jesus, . . . *not my will, but thine, be done* (Luke 22:42). The truth of this stated affirmation will obliterate one's sense of personality, personal power, false pride, and the personal sense of ability; for he is now earnestly desirous of God's guidance and reward, as well as lovingly waiting on Him to have the matter worked out in God's own time and way . . . *then do we with patience wait for it. Likewise the Spirit also helpeth our infirmities* (Romans 8:25, 26).

Let us take another trend of thought, and use as an illustration, one in search of employment. I find one under these circumstances needs to understand, know and realize that his position and work, as well as his reward for good and faithful service, is in the divine Mind here and now; not going to be, but is a present reality. And as he goes forth in loving humility, obediently following not his own human will and desire in the matter, but the gentle leadings of Truth and Love, he has a right to know and hold steadfastly to the fact that Love is leading him in the way he should go, and into the work and position for which he is best fitted to do the most good. *I* [God] *will instruct thee and teach thee in the way which thou shalt go: I will guide thee with mine eye* [intelligence] (Psalms 32:8).

Should the impression—the *still small voice*—seem not to appear readily, the seeker is counselled to *Fear not,* nor worry, nor yet sit idly by, but watchfully *wait on God,* and in doing so, continuing to prayerfully seek Truth in studying his Bible and the Christian Science textbook; stilling the tempest of the so-called mortal mind with the thought that *I and my Father are one* (Mind and Its reflection); and knowing Love never fails, no matter what the suggestion of delay may try to make one believe, but realizing that God's time is now.

I find people often wonder why they have to wait for their problems to work out; why the postponement of the harmony sought after. You may be certain it is for some good purpose. It may be to test the sincerity of your desire to have things really work out in God's way. It may be to teach you patience; but more likely it is to have you honestly examine yourself and see your own mental condition so that you may realize what a brood of vipers you are still harboring—consciously or unconsciously,—such as fear, doubt, impatience, fretfulness, peevishness, bitterness, or resentment because things do not work out in your way. It may be because of selfishness—doing what you are engaged in for what you personally may acquire out of it,—forgetting that the highest and best service is wholly unselfish, and looking to see how much good your service will bring your brother-man: selfwill, self-justification, self-righteousness, self-pity, envy, jealousy, temper, hate, malice, lust, licentiousness, perhaps revenge, covetousness, stubbornness, and a determination to have your own instead of God's way: or yet, to uncover a tenacious holding to mortal man and matter as your substance and supply.

One does not always understand and realize what an unprepared and seething mental condition he may be in, until he is put to some test which will uncover the wickedness of his own heart through a seeming delay and a period of waiting; but it must be apparent to all right and honest thinking people, that one can never build safely on such a false foundation as this. Neither can he work out his problem in God's way and be able to render the right kind of service when in this ungodlike mental condition. One must first be made ready, and then the way will open and he will find his rightful place and reward.

Even the apostles had to become ready. Some one, in defense, may exclaim: But they were to do God's work! True, but is not all good and legitimate work God's work? Of course it is. Jesus said: *And the King shall answer and say unto them, Verily I say unto you, Inasmuch as ye have done it unto one of the least of these my brethren, ye have done it unto me* (Matt. 25:40).

Hence it is not for one to criticize God or man for the seeming delay, or explode mentally because things do not come as fast or work out according to one's preconceived sense of things; but it is to put his finger on his lips, enter into his closet alone with God, and permitting God to reveal unto him what is the first and most important thing for him to do: then do it immediately, with God looking on, as it were. He will no doubt find that when he surrenders his human will to God and lets God rule, he will find his place and work awaiting him, and Love will lead him into it and be his *exceeding great reward* (Gen. 15:1).

When the impression or the divine leadings come to take certain human footsteps, follow them, trusting God implicitly as to the outcome, knowing full well that God never fails. He will bring to pass whatever is for your good and the good of all concerned.

Again, one may be employed. He may be selling a commodity, but seems to be at a loss in knowing to whom to go. He may also fear to call upon anyone—pride may have much to do with it; his line seems beneath him. Under such circumstances he needs to know that God, divine Mind, guides him; and that it is divine Love who opens the way as well as prepares him to see the party or parties he is guided to call upon. If he has abandoned his own selfishness in the matter, and conscientiously and lovingly seeks his own in his brother's good, desiring to do unto others as he would have them do unto himself, he need have no fear concerning the outcome, because he is looking to God, infinite Mind, as his sure and unfailing reward. He is now earnestly endeavoring to take the human footsteps at Mind's behest.

One should be most careful that he is not mis-led into counting upon what might be the financial reward, but should banish it; neither should he out-line. He should not even be dismayed if nothing apparently comes of his first meeting, knowing that God is his reward in God's own way, yea, his sub-stance and supply. He can expect his reward because it is God's law, just the same as when one labors with a problem in mathematics and is re-warded with the answer. *And the Lord shall guide thee continually, and satisfy thy soul in drought, and make fat thy bones: and thou shalt be like a watered garden, and like a spring of water, whose waters fail not* (Isaiah 58:11).

It must be plain to all careful thinkers that true service rests upon the right motive and love animat-ing every action or endeavor in behalf of those over us, associated with us, or those under our authority, as well as those with whom we seem to contact in our daily lives, whether business or social.

God does not always work miracles to convince a man of what he should do. He works more through the "still small voice"—the gentle leadings of Spirit,—which in turn fills one's consciousness with peace, assurance, and a confidence that he is moving according to Principle.

If one is not at peace in his movements, he had better endeavor anew to surrender unconditionally to God, and further watchfully wait on divine Mind to show the next step to take: this is imperative. If man moves before God designates the way, it leads him into confusion and ends in failure. But not so, when he turns to and lovingly waits on God.

Two great characters in Biblical history are shining examples of what this true serving embodies.

Moses, living and surrounded by the greatest of so-called material substance and splendor, had to depart from the courts of Egypt and become a sheep herder before he was lifted higher. Daniel, a prince in his own country, became a captive slave before being exalted. Your human efforts, guided by God, Mind, if done lovingly, constitute service: and God is the rewarder.

I have found it to be infallibly certain and the reward sure, that when one looks to Mind to guide his human efforts, if put into practice constantly, it will lead him into the abundance of all good provided by God, and placed by Him within the reach of every man, woman, and child who is willing to lovingly enter into and dwell in "the secret place of the Most High" and rely on God—Principle—absolutely. Amos says, *He* [God] *revealeth his secret unto his servants:* likewise David declared: *The secret of the Lord is with them that fear* [love] *him: and he will shew them his covenant,* viz., promises—God's law of fulfillment. *His secret is with the righteous,* saith the wise man.

St. Paul brings it out in these words: *Now to him that is of power to stablish you according to my gospel, and the preaching of Jesus Christ, according to the revelation of the mystery, which was kept secret since the world began, But now is made manifest, and by the scriptures of the prophets, according to the commandment of the everlasting God, made known to all nations for the obedience of faith* (Rom. 16:25).

It is an infallible law of Mind that the idea (man) that knows and realizes his at-one-ment with the Mind that is all, and ever active in Its manifestation, cannot fail to demonstrate the symbol needed to meet the human sense of need.

Summing up the Scriptural basis upon which substance and supply is understood and demonstrated, and the conclusions my long study, practice, and efforts have verified by the fruit borne, shows me that the success of one's efforts must be founded upon and proceed from

UNDERSTANDING,
OBEDIENCE,
RELIANCE.

To amplify the subject more fully, I will repeat, that in my experience I have become thoroughly convinced that this demonstration is based upon a clearer, higher, fuller, more comprehensive and correct understanding of God, of man's oneness with God, an absolute and loving obedience to, and a complete, unconditional and unreserved reliance upon the Principle of all being,—God.

Christ not only furnished the key to God's infinite storehouse of all good, but was and is himself the door. All must enter through him: that is, live the life of understanding and realization exemplified by Jesus, the fruit of which produced immediate supply of whatever was needed, and whenever needed.

As one who wishes to demonstrate the science of higher mathematics in figuring out a geometrical problem, for instance, must of necessity first gain a clearer, fuller, higher, more comprehensive and correct understanding of, be obedient to, and rely absolutely and unreservedly upon the principle which underlies the science of mathematics, even so he must gain a like understanding of, be obedient to, and absolutely rely upon God, the Principle of his substance and supply. There is no other way.

Let me here add, and let the reader analyze it for himself, to-wit, that God, Mind, is the Principle of the science of mathematics. (We are not speaking of numbers; they are but the humanly employed symbols used in obtaining a result. God, Mind, knows the answer before its inception.) This science partakes of the nature of God, is a fixed or unchangeable fact, and is eternal and perfect. God being All, and in all, the correct application of mathematics, and the right answer, are one, and can be nothing other than the demonstration of the unchanging nature of God,—Principle in expression.

The solution of the seeming problem of supply, then, requires the same understanding, obedience, and reliance, with as scientific a certainty of solution as does the mathematical with its correct demonstration. They are but different states of mental activity in the one, all-inclusive Principle.

Mathematics is used every day by mortals with perfect results; but how few ever give thought to like perfect results in their daily lives and supply; yet the same Principle is just as applicable and the results just as perfect.

I find that evil has not only blinded mankind generally to this vital fact, but the Christian as well. The reason for this sad condition lies in the error and false belief entertained about God's promised and demonstrated mercy. This in turn has led all mankind to believe that it was not so imperative to be one hundred per cent obedient to God, the Principle of all being, as he has learned through experience, correct teaching and understanding is the case in working out his mathematical problems, be they ever so simple or complex. Today he knows and realizes that there is no other way; consequently he yields to it obediently and conscientiously. When man likewise reaches this point in demonstrating the truth of his being, he will find it simple enough to demonstrate substance and supply, for he will then discover that it works just as positively and automatically as two plus two are four.

He will no longer be misled by the false, erroneous belief about God's promised and demonstrated mercy, for he will now awake and realize that God does not overlook his sins, be they wilful, or sins of ignorance; and furthermore, he will finally learn through bitter experience, if need be, and through a corrected understanding, that there is no more discounting of poor and incorrect work in working out his salvation than there is in working out his problem in mathematics. He will find that God's mercy does not consist in overlooking his sins, but in this, that God lovingly bears with him and extends unto man an ever available opportunity to truly repent and correct his mistakes, his false and erroneous beliefs of every name and nature.

God so loved man that He sent His only begotten son into the world to save mankind, and to show man how to obey Him perfectly and absolutely; furthermore God always stands ready to aid and enable him to keep His commandments which is in fact *the whole duty of man.* But this does not mean that God takes down His standard of perfection nor lessens man's responsibility to abide therein. Sooner or later, here or hereafter, man will realize that he must be fully obedient; for his obedience is demanded of him just as much as it was of Abraham when *The Lord appeared unto Abram, and said, . . . I am the Almighty God; walk before me, and be thou perfect* (Gen. 17:1). Christ's command is just as emphatic: *Be ye therefore perfect, even as your Father which is in heaven is perfect* (Matt. 5:48). *But let patience have her perfect work, that ye may be perfect and entire, wanting nothing,* counsels the Apostle James.

I am deeply grateful to God for my early Christian training, that I was led to seek, find and enjoy God's will concerning my every movement and effort, and that I was early shown it was necessary for me to be lovingly obedient unto God, because it was just and right, and not because of fear of punishment. I am happy to say that never once have I found that God asked me to do anything or to take any step except it was for His glory, my good, and the good of mankind. And it has always been true that He only required of me to take but one step at a time, and only as fast as I saw it and understood it as the leading of divine Mind.

I am also deeply thankful to my heavenly Father that I was early taught and made to realize it was most imperative to be honest with God, just as I found it necessary for me to be honest, conscientious, and faithful to the principle underlying the science of mathematics.

Furthermore, I cannot be too grateful to divine Love for teaching me, and proving to me in so many ways in daily life, how God cared for me in the minutest details. I learned to lovingly depend on Him and realize that He always met my human needs, and never came too late. I have often experienced, and I trust I have been taught the lesson which God, through Moses, taught the children of Israel,—to trust Him day by day; and as Josiah Conden aptly worded a hymn:

> "Day by day the manna fell,
> Oh, to learn this lesson well."

In studying this experience of the chosen Children of God, I found they had to be obedient, and look steadfastly to God for daily supply; nor were they to worry or gather for the morrow, except in the case where God Himself commanded them to do so on the sixth day that they might have sufficient manna on their Sabbath without going out and gathering it.

When the Israelites, in their desert wanderings, retired at night their cupboards were bare: they had nothing visible or tangible as food for the following day. They had to learn through experience and obedience that they must not only trust God implicitly, but also do it lovingly and in the spirit of humility and obedience; and when they did this, they never knew what lack was. Later, when they became sufficiently advanced in their understanding of the infinite supply of all good, and continued to be obedient, they found their storehouses filled and their wine presses bursting with new wine.

This I have found, through my many years of demonstrating substance and supply on a purely metaphysical basis, to be the case in meeting my daily needs, be they ever so small or great; for I have learned that this omnipresent and omnipotent Principle—God—is not only equal to every case or condition, but He is ever willing to supply all my needs.

The primal desire of the seeker after substance, however, must not be that of seeking the kingdom of God for material gain, but conversely seek to gain the true understanding of God, the Principle underlying the substance and supply of all good, that he may visibly, as well as mentally, express the essence of God, Life, in harmonious existence, the only manifestation that God is aware of or created . . . *thou shalt remember the Lord thy God: for it is he that giveth thee power to get wealth, that he may establish his covenant which he sware unto thy fathers, as it is this day* (Deut. 8:18).

Let the reader take heed of the three essentials before mentioned, namely, Understanding, Obedience, Reliance, if he sincerely desires to enjoy the Life that is God, and of God, and try to gain the knowledge fundamentally required. In conclusion let us take note of some Scriptural enlightenment and promises, as well as of a few individuals who exemplified their knowledge of these essentials.

The wise man wrote: *Happy is the man that findeth wisdom, and the man that getteth understanding. For the merchandise of it is better than the merchandise of silver, and the gain thereof than fine gold. She is more precious than rubies: and all the things thou canst desire are not to be compared unto her. Length of days is in her right hand; and in her left hand riches and honour. Her ways are ways of pleasantness, and all her paths are peace. She is a tree of life to them that lay hold upon her: and happy is every one that retaineth her* (Prov. 3:13-18).

King Solomon stands as a striking example of the wisdom of seeking and choosing understanding above all else. In the first chapter of Second Chronicles we read: *In that night did God appear unto Solomon, and said unto him, Ask what I shall give thee. And Solomon said unto God ... Give me now wisdom and knowledge, ... And God said to Solomon, Because this was in thine heart, and thou hast not asked riches, wealth, or honour, ... but hast asked wisdom and knowledge for thyself, ... Wisdom and knowledge is granted unto thee; and I will give thee riches, and wealth, and honour.*

The foregoing quotation illustrates the abundant inflow of substance to one seeking "the kingdom," that is, the correct understanding of God.

It includes in itself not only salvation from evil of every sort, but it also includes true substance or riches, honour, dominion, and power as well. Consequently the Scriptures emphasize the requirement that *in all thy getting, get understanding* first of all.

Jesus said, *But seek ye first the kingdom* [understanding] *of God and his righteousness; and all these things shall be added unto you.* Seeking and gaining the true understanding of God discloses man's oneness with his heavenly Father. Jesus' teachings divulge this truth, as note, *I and my Father are one* (John 10:31). *Neither pray I for these alone, but for them also which shall believe . . . That they all may be one; as thou, Father, art in me, and I in thee, that they also may be one in us* (John 17:20, 21).

The second fundamental is Obedience; obedience to God and His Commandments. Loving obedience is a sure and unfailing entrance into, and the realization of all good, and the good spoken of and so clearly set forth in Deuteronomy. *And it shall come to pass, if thou shalt hearken diligently unto the voice of the Lord thy God, to observe and to do all His commandments which I command thee this day . . . Blessed shalt thou be in the city, and blessed shalt thou be in the field. Blessed shall be the fruit of thy body, and the fruit of thy ground, and the fruit of thy cattle, the increase of thy kine, and the flocks of thy sheep. Blessed shall be thy basket and thy store. Blessed shalt thou be when thou comest in, and blessed shalt thou be when thou goest out . . . The Lord shall command the blessing upon thee in thy store-houses, and in all that thou settest thine hand unto; . . . if thou shalt keep the commandments of the Lord thy God, and walk in his ways. . . . And the Lord shall make thee plenteous in goods, . . . The Lord shall open unto thee his good treasure, the heaven to give the rain unto thy land in his season, and to bless all the work of thine hand: and thou shalt lend unto many nations, and thou shalt not borrow* (Deut. 28:1-12). Can one ask for more?

Finally, Reliance: for an unconditional and an unreserved reliance on God, Spirit, the Principle of man's being, will invariably cause man to realize His presence, and the abundance of all good provided by infinite Love for each and every one of His children who understands, faithfully and lovingly obeys, and relies wholly on the one and only source of all real good—God.

Abraham, "the father of the faithful," stands forth as a beautiful example of one who had gained this true understanding of God, lovingly obeyed

Him implicitly and relied on Him unreservedly, when he departed, at God's command, to a country of which he knew not. And again, when he was called upon to offer up Isaac, the seed of the promise.

Daniel stands as another illustration. He demonstrated out of poverty, bondage, and even the lion's den into freedom, honor, dominion, and riches by his understanding of God and his oneness with the Father, loving obedience to, and his unreserved reliance on God.

In our own time I find that Mrs. Eddy stands out before the Christian world of today as the highest exemplification of the Scriptural teachings on this subject through her wonderful understanding of this divine Principle, her faithful and loving obedience to God, and an unreserved reliance upon Him, which lifted her up and out of seeming obscurity and limitation into becoming the world renowned Discoverer and Founder of Christian Science, and the recognized Leader of the most remarkable religious movement since the time of Christ; and who amply demonstrated that when one really and truly seeks the kingdom of God first of all, all good will flow into his life.

Not only did she demonstrate understanding, obedience, reliance, honor, and riches, but she stands as an example for all time to her followers, of wisdom and intelligence, poise, grace, sweetness, humility, modesty, faithfulness to God, His cause, mankind and her own kin. She so wisely arranged for the use of the fruits of her faithfulness to God and mankind, after she had generously provided for her own, that she was enabled to dedicate for all time her ever increasing substance, which God was and is continually pouring in upon her estate, to the promulgation of her teachings, and the faithful protection and spread of Christian Science throughout the whole world.

Thus we see that God's infinite storehouse of all good is open to every one who will but comply with God's simple and reasonable requirements. We will also discover that there is more than enough for each and every one of God's children, just as there is enough of the principle and numbers of mathematics; and when we appropriate all we need, we will find that we do not rob our neighbor of anything; neither does our neighbor, who appropriates what God provides for him, rob us of anything good or limit us in any way. The supply is infinite for each and every one, and there is no exception, nor is God a respecter of persons. Every one is invited: every one can enter: and every one is urged by divine Love to come unto the feast of all good—the bridal feast of the Lamb of God.

I am deeply grateful to Mrs. Eddy for this enlightened thought wherein she revealed that the Scriptures, when correctly understood, set forth in the Old and New Testaments the recipe for the healing of all the ills mortal man or human flesh is heir to, be it that of the individual, family, church, or state. This Biblical recipe is concise and to the point in every instance needed, simple and so plain that *the wayfaring men, though fools, shall not err therein,* but may understand and apply it successfully; and when understood, one begins to realize that it is omnipresent, as God is the author of it, in fact is God; hence it is free to all as is God's mercy and sunshine. It has been recorded and revealed by God's prophets, His only begotten Son—Jesus the Christ, and his apostles.

This all-sufficient recipe of God is summarized and condensed into one single word—the greatest word known to all mankind—

LOVE.

Christ was and is the embodiment, the personification, the essence, yea, the full expression of everpresent Love. He it is that is the remedy in action.

God is love, said the Apostle John, who understood this recipe; and Love, God's synonym, reveals the substance and essence embodied in the supply of all good to man, Love's image, instantly available. It was Jesus' understanding of the Christ, *who being the effulgence of his* [God's] *glory, and the very image of his* [Love's] *substance* (Heb. 1:3, Revised Version), was the only realization Jesus considered or acknowledged, and which enabled him to supply the need as the need appeared. Through this knowledge of his at-one-ment with Love, Jesus immediately supplied wine for the wedding feast, food for the multitudes in the wilderness, money for temple taxes, and restored the dead to their sorrowing families. Is it not plain that God, divine Love, would, and in fact does supply to His own image and likeness, man, all available good that He, Himself, has created to be expressed? There is certainly no love expressed in lack and limitation, want and woe. Then such seeming situations are godless, and being godless or loveless, they have no existence in reality.

In addition to all that has been set forth as to the abundance of substance and supply ever available for man, the one eager to regain his birthright may question himself as to what sort of prayer will yield such an effulgent existence; for even the devout Christian with his imploring and pleading prayer to God, has found that many of his appeals have remained unanswered, and of a consequence believes it to be the will of God that he suffer a continuance of the situation or condition. The basis or cause of this type of prayer is the belief in a separateness from God or good, and is not the prayer of joyous affirmation and exultation, even in the face of seeming insurmountable obstacles, that one with the knowledge of his oneness with God utters and rejoices over because of his understanding of divine Love, and the inseparableness of man, the image, from his God, the Creator of all good only.

I have cause for much gratitude to God for leading me, through the study of the Scriptures and the teachings of Christian Science, into a better, a more comprehensive knowledge of prayer based on an understanding of God and man's oneness with Him. True prayer, I find, is a prayer of affirmation and of confidence—an affirmation of God's power and presence, and confidence in the reality of God's goodness and love instantly available.

To define more adequately, true prayer consists of an honest and sincere desire to flee from evil, coupled with an earnest longing to know God aright; being enabled to recognize His will and do it; to understand our at-one-ment with Him; possessed of a clear realization that God has not only provided all good for us, but has given it all to us through his Son, the one Christ, as exemplified by Jesus; and, too, a fearless affirmation of our birthright, all of which necessitates a loving yet radical and unreserved reliance on God. Here we must learn to stand until the answer is made manifest in God's own way and time; conscious, however, that God's time is always the eternal now, and the truth of our affirmations is a reality now.

This is illustrated in many of the books of both the Old and New Testament, and especially so in the Psalms, wherein we find many examples of this form of acknowledging the infinite affluence of God. Take the Twenty-third Psalm of only six verses. David's prayer of affirmation and confidence covered almost a score of ideas paramount to his well-being and happiness, all of them he sought in, and knew that he had them from God, divine Love. David acknowledged God as his Shepherd; he knew he possessed God's leadership or guidance: and the rest of the Psalm declared David the recipient of confidence, contentment, rest, peace, healing, understanding, protection, destruction of fear, consolation, assurance, provision, honor, super-abundance, goodness and mercy, home or harmony. Coupling this with the Ninety-first Psalm we have a prayer of affirmation that covers all conceivable situations or conditions humanity seems to face.

The Twenty-third and Ninety-first Psalms are, no doubt, read and studied more than any other two chapters in the whole Bible; but how many of the Bible students really realize that these Psalms conjoined were David's prayer of affirmation? They do not contain a single word of pleading. It is purely a declaration, an humble, loving and unfaltering affirmation that God supplied him under the most trying circumstances with all good needful, and is exhibitive of his unreserved and radical reliance upon the infinite I AM. I know from personal experience that if a student will come into the same understanding, and faithfully love and obey God, holding steadfastly to the affirmations contained in these Psalms until they become so thoroughly the truth, the reality, to his own consciousness, he will be the recipient of all good the same as David.

One of the greatest, yet exceedingly brief prayers of affirmation and supreme confidence is that of Jesus at the tomb of Lazarus. *Father, I thank thee that thou hast heard me. And I knew that thou hearest me always: but because of the people which stand by I said it, that they may believe that thou hast sent me* (John 11: 41, 42). It also illustrates the supreme power of the prayer of affirmation to overcome even the power of death, when based on the foundation on which this prayer of Jesus rested, namely, the understanding of God; the realization of his at-one-ment with the Father; the surrender of his own will to the will of God, or an absolute obedience to, and an unreserved and radical reliance on God.

Jesus, with his clear understanding, absolute reliance, perfect obedience, and with a knowledge of man's at-one-ment with God, gave to us these instructions: *Therefore I say unto you, All things whatsoever ye pray and ask for, believe that ye have received them and we shall have them* (Revised Version), an enlightenment, clearly defining our at-one-ment with everything needful—a reflection of the infinite storehouse of God. Then ask yourself this question, How can I lack any good thing when I am one with the Father? Atonement, or at-one-ment, is my forever inseparable existence with substance and supply of every name and nature, which is God.

Sometimes, I find myself wondering how many people there are who really realize the importance and the power there is in these three essentials— understanding, affirmation and reliance—when it comes to the one and only avenue we possess to bring our consciousness into its rightful relationship to our dear heavenly Father,—that of prayer.

Many, on first becoming interested in Christian Science, and finding the Truth so at variance with their former beliefs, are at a loss for the moment in really understanding how to pray aright. They readily see that it is not for them to plead, as of old, with God to give them what they need from day to day, any more than they have to plead with the principle of mathematics to make two and two equal four; for Truth has enlightened their consciousness with the understanding that God has already provided all good for each and every one of His children; and not only that, but He has already given it to them, if they will only obey Him and accept His blessings. Yet they realize the need of coming to their God in prayer. Just the mode of righteous prayer is not grasped all at once; but as they progress in their understanding of Christian Science, and continue to study the Scriptures in their true light, they soon find their own prayers taking form in like manner, and with as satisfying an assurance, as David's prayers of affirmation found in the book of Psalms, and especially in the Twenty-third and Ninety-first; also our Master's mode of prayer and his way of approaching his Father and our Father.

The Scriptures tell us that *The prayer of a righteous* [right-thinking] *man availeth much.* And assuredly righteous prayer produces countless spiritual realities of unspeakable joy and peace, mentally entertained in one's own consciousness, ever enlarging in scope and sustaining man far beyond the world's conception of sustenance. In addition, the externalized symbols of spiritual ideas become apparent to meet the human sense of need commensurate with man's understanding of and his tenacious, steadfast and unswerving holding to the truth underlying his prayer of affirmation that God is their source and the manifestation thereof here and now. *For we are made partakers of Christ* [Truth], *if we hold the beginning of our confidence stedfast unto the end* (Hebrews 3:14).

There is untold joy in store for the one who gains this knowledge; for true substance and supply includes every spiritual idea in the infinite storehouse of God, Mind, the manifestation of which entertained symbolically or mentally, makes up our happiness, peace, and contentment; and the manifestation of these shows God's presence with us,— that we rightly understand true prayer.

In this affirmative form of prayer there is no pleading or agonizing appeals to God, any more than to the principle of mathematics, for that which man, by his very oneness or relationship, is already endowed with as God's image. Rather is it a joyful acknowledgment of God's allness, and of man's birthright to everything needful for harmonious existence. True prayer is rest, a surcease from the suggestions that assail one's consciousness with temptation to believe evil's intimations as real; for it is affirming and realizing our understanding that harmonious, infinite Mind permits of no other activity than that which emanates from Himself. This prayer of understanding faith by man leaves the responsibility of deliverance and safe-keeping with God. *Come unto me, all ye that labour and are heavy laden, and I will give you rest.*

Let no man condemn himself for the past, but recognize his errors, and honestly turn from his own evil ways; for God, Love, is of purer eyes than to behold evil. Rather let him listen to the endearing offer God puts forth to all His children through the prophet Isaiah: *Come now, and let us reason together, saith the Lord: though your sins be as scarlet, they shall be as white as snow; though they be red like crimson, they shall be as wool. If ye be willing and obedient, ye shall eat the good of the land.* Surely no better proffer can God make to man than this one wherein He promises purity and the abundance of all good.

All that God has asked of us or is asking of us, is that we accept him whom He sent into the world—the world of false understanding concerning God and His image and likeness, man,—and known as Jesus the Christ, who portrayed to humanity by his word and works that which is God's image, or man: also that we pattern our lives after him and gain the same understanding exemplified by Jesus.

God has supplied us with His recipes—prescribed means—which are fundamentally the very essence of Himself, and which we, by our affirmation and realization of the truth of our affirmation, find, are expressed or demonstrated by us as God's own image or reflection. This supply of the substance of Himself, together with the true, earthly existence portrayed by Jesus to illustrate the power embodied therein, is the light shining in the darkness of materialistic beliefs for us to comprehend, realize, and utilize. It can be attained by everyone, and we can joyfully look forward to the success of our efforts by these words of Jesus, *Verily, verily, I say unto you, He that believeth on me, the works that I do shall he do also; and greater works than these shall he do; because I go unto my Father* (John 14:12).

I find the more I study them and obey or put this form of applying God's promises—laws—into practice, the more I realize my freedom from error, my true liberty as a son of God and my birthright and protection as a child of God.

God has an infinite number of channels through which good flows into the consciousness, life, and experience of the man who understands, lovingly obeys, and fully relies upon God as his substance and supply. Does not God, through the prophet

Isaiah, tell us that . . . *in the wilderness shall water break out, and streams in the desert,* illustrating that God's infinite storehouse of channels and streams of good are omnipresent even in the face of the suggestion that one is in the wilderness of lack and limitation? These channels, I have found, are always open, clear, and free from all the debris of sin, disease, death, lack, limitation, want and woe, and are filled with every idea of good needful to man; and not only that but our dear heavenly Father guides, directs, sustains, and abundantly blesses our every effort put forth in the spirit of humility, obedience, love, unselfishness, and in doing unto others as we would have them do unto us.

Therefore let one keep his consciousness so filled with this clear understanding of God, a realization of his oneness with Him, obedience to God, and with such an unreserved reliance on Him, that fear, doubt, worry, lack and limitation of anything good cannot enter. Here stand! and as St. Paul says, *Having done all, to stand,* lovingly and steadfastly looking to God. Standing in this atmosphere of spiritual existence and oneness with the Father, one will surely realize something of what this scientific mental condition and abidance therein will do for him in bringing into his life day by day the affluence of all good needful. For God, the giver of all good, is ever present, and is the same tender, loving Father-Mother God who has set before us His infinite storehouse of unlimited ALL, and is calling and beckoning each and every one to enter here and now.

It is self-evident that inasmuch as God is man's protection, neither man nor devil (evil) can delay, hinder, or prevent all good from flowing into the consciousness and life of man, because infinite Love provides and protects both the channel and the inflow of ever present good, be it that of life, health, strength, peace, joy, love, courage, ambition, steadfastness, opportunity, or success. Yea, the substance and supply of every name and nature needful. Remember this: it is man alone who always hinders, retards, or limits God's blessings and supply from flowing into his life.

Commensurate with man's understanding and realization of God's goodness and supply, together with the fact that God is omnipresent, omnipotent, and omniscient, will he be led to see, understand, and realize that nothing can interfere with the inflow of everything man needs from day to day. Neither can this inflow of all good be subverted or diverted.

I have further found that by holding humbly, lovingly, obediently and steadfastly to the great truth above set forth, God's promise that no good thing will He withhold from them that love and faithfully obey Him, is the truth, yea, is God's unchangeable, eternal law.

You will find, too, that in proportion as you are prepared by divine Love to perceive, accept, appreciate, and utilize substance correctly, God will abundantly supply you with ideas of substance, which, in turn, will be made manifest to your consciousness and understanding in a form, measure, and character you will be able to comprehend and utilize. Thus you will realize that divine Love provides all good for you here and now in abundantly meeting your every human need.

Behold, I have set before thee an open door, and no man can shut it (Revelation).

Our Loving Father-Mother God, Omnipotent, All-harmonious: We Thank Thee that Thou Art Our Everpresent Life, Truth, Love, Substance, and Intelligence; Our Health, Strength, Joy, Peace and Harmony: Our Salvation and Protection From All Evil, and Our Supply of All Good, Through Christ — Truth.

CHAPTER XII

ARTICLE

LACK AND LIMITATION UNKNOWN TO GOD

THE ONLY POWER   I wish you would sit quietly and MEDITATE upon the great fact that God is OMNIPRESENT — fills all space — is the only power and the only presence — is the ALL-IN-ALL of all things. Get this clearly before your mind, please, and know that such a thing as lack and limitation is not known to God — does not exist in His kingdom — and you know His kingdom is omnipresent. It is the only kingdom there is.

> *"Finally, my brethren, be strong in the*
> *Lord, and in the power of his might."*
> (Ephesians 6:10)